THE MENOPAUSE FRAMEWORK

Proven Strategies for Building a Thriving Women's Health Practice

CURT WARNER

ISBN: 978-1-7346866-1-6

Published by:
Platinum Media Solutions
Charlotte, NC
704.200.2239

PlatinumMediaSolutions.com

CONTENTS

Preface... 1

Dedication 3

Chapter 1: The Untapped Potential of Menopause Care – A Golden
Opportunity for Medical Professionals 5

Chapter 2: Fundamentals of Business Growth............................... 17

Chapter 3: Evaluating Your Practice so You Never Waste Money on
Ineffective Programs Again 43

Chapter 4: Positioning Yourself as the Expert in Women's Health and
Menopause Treatments... 67

Chapter 5: Expanding Your Reach: A Comprehensive Guide to Traffic
Generation and Brand Building 89

Chapter 6: Embracing Sales in Women's Health: A Gentle Approach 97

Chapter 7: Increasing Sales Through Strategic Client Engagement . 109

Chapter 8: Referrals 121

Chapter 9: Building Strategic Alliances to Grow Your Women's Health
Practice 131

Chapter 10: Bringing It All Together – Your Roadmap to a Thriving
Menopause Practice.. 141

Resources 147

PREFACE

When I founded The Menopause Association, a question often surfaced: Why would a man with over 30 years of experience in marketing and business development... spanning industries as varied as real estate, mortgage, law, wealth management, retail, and more... turn his focus to menopause care? The answer is deeply personal yet universally resonant. It begins with my wife, Kari, whose struggles with menopause... debilitating headaches, mood swings, insomnia, and a pervasive sense of aging... revealed a silent crisis affecting millions of women. Despite a wealth of advanced treatments, she faced a healthcare system offering little guidance, leaving her to endure needless suffering. That wasn't just a wake-up call; it was a catalyst for action.

My career has been a tapestry of turning vision into value. I've established and successfully exited multiple companies, including a high eight-figure deal, leveraging my expertise to build thriving enterprises across diverse fields. Over the past decade, I've channeled this entrepreneurial acumen into empowering medical professionals in anti-aging, longevity, and regenerative medicine, guiding them to create cash-based practices that redefine patient care and profitability. Yet, Kari's ordeal illuminated a glaring gap in menopause care: a lack of directed support, education, and access to life-changing solutions. I realized the same proven strategies... expertise, innovation, and a relentless commitment to results... that fueled my successes could bridge this divide. Thus, The Menopause Association, a 501(c)(3) nonprofit, was born to inform, educate, and empower women navigating this pivotal life stage, while equipping providers with tools to lead.

This book extends that mission. The Menopause Framework isn't just a guide; it's a roadmap to transform menopause care into a thriving, compassionate specialty. Drawing from over three decades of experience across a plethora of industries, I've distilled strategies that have built empires... now tailored to the unique opportunity of women's health. Within these pages, you'll find practical steps to position yourself as an expert, attract loyal patients, and grow your practice geometrically, addressing an underserved market crying out for leadership. From crafting Signature Solutions to forging strategic alliances, this book equips you to turn passion into a lasting legacy.

Menopause transcends gender... it's a human issue. Kari's journey taught me that empathy and action can redefine this chapter from struggle to strength. As founder of The Menopause Association (https://menopauseassociation.org), I've seen how connecting women with skilled providers changes lives. This book is my invitation to you... forward-thinking practitioners in longevity, anti-aging, and beyond... to join this movement. Together, we can elevate care, empower women to thrive, and build practices that endure. The opportunity is vast, the need urgent, and the potential yours to seize. Let's redefine menopause care, one patient, one practice, one community at a time.

Curt Warner
Founder, The Menopause Association
CEO, Platinum Media Solutions

DEDICATION

To Kari, my love and my inspiration… your strength through the challenges of menopause lit the spark for this journey. This book is for you and for every woman navigating this transformative chapter of their lives, seeking the care and confidence you deserve.

To the medical professionals who dare to lead… may you find in these pages the tools to build thriving practices and a legacy of empowerment for women everywhere.

And to The Menopause Association community… your stories, resilience, and trust fuel this mission to redefine menopause care. Together, we're turning a silent struggle into a vibrant new beginning.

With gratitude and purpose,
Curt Warner

CHAPTER 1

THE UNTAPPED POTENTIAL OF MENOPAUSE CARE – A GOLDEN OPPORTUNITY FOR MEDICAL PROFESSIONALS

In the evolving landscape of healthcare, one segment of the population remains critically underserved: women transitioning through menopause. This chapter explores the compelling reasons why focusing on women's health, particularly menopause care, presents an unprecedented opportunity for medical professionals seeking to establish or expand their cash-based practices.

THE MENOPAUSE MARKET: A VAST AND GROWING OPPORTUNITY

The menopause transition affects millions of women worldwide, yet the healthcare system has largely failed to address their unique needs. Consider these striking statistics:

- By 2025, the number of postmenopausal women worldwide is expected to exceed 1 billion.

- In the United States alone, more than 1 million women experience menopause each year.

- Approximately 6,000 women in the U.S. reach menopause daily.

- The global menopause market was valued at $15.4 billion in 2021 and is projected to reach $24.4 billion by 2030.

These figures reveal a vast, untapped patient base, highlighting the urgency for menopause-focused care. However, the current healthcare system is ill-equipped to meet their needs. A survey by the American Association of Retired Persons found that only 1 in 5 women in the U.S. received a referral to a menopause specialist, and of the 60% of women who seek medical attention, an alarming 75% are left untreated.

THE IMPACT OF MENOPAUSE ON WOMEN'S LIVES

Far more than a biological shift, menopause reshapes women's lives, profoundly affecting women's quality of life, careers, and relationships. Research highlights the following issues:

- 80% of surveyed women reported difficulty managing menopausal symptoms while on the job.

- 72% felt uneasy or self-conscious when experiencing symptoms like brain fog at work.

- Untreated menopause symptoms cost about $1.8 billion in lost working time each year in the U.S.

- Menopausal women spend 45% more on healthcare costs annually compared to non-menopausal women.

The most common symptoms affecting women include:

- Vasomotor symptoms (hot flashes, night sweats)

- Sleep disturbances

- Mood changes and depression

- Cognitive issues ("brain fog")

- Genitourinary symptoms (vaginal dryness, urinary issues)

- Sexual health concerns

- Bone density loss

These symptoms can persist for years, significantly impacting a woman's personal and professional life. Yet, many women suffer in silence due to lack of awareness, stigma, or inadequate healthcare options.

Beyond the human cost lies a compelling business case ... one that savvy practitioners can seize.

THE REVENUE POTENTIAL FOR MENOPAUSE-FOCUSED PRACTICES

For medical professionals considering a focus on menopause care, the revenue potential is substantial. While specific figures can vary based on location, services offered, and practice model, consider these indicators:

- The average annual healthcare expense for menopausal women is $1,243 per member, compared to $848 for the general population. This number is substantially higher for women who seek medical assistance outside traditional sources, such as with their Primary Care Physician or OB/GYN.

- Women using hormone replacement therapy (HRT) have 11% lower overall healthcare costs compared to women using other menopause therapies.

- The global women's health market was estimated at nearly $41.5 billion in 2022, with a forecasted compound annual growth rate of over 5% from 2023 through 2030.

By offering comprehensive, personalized menopause care, practices can create long-term, high-ticket packages, which may include a combination of:

- Initial comprehensive evaluations
- Ongoing hormone therapy management
- Regular health screenings
- Lifestyle and nutrition counseling
- Weight management
- Incontinence treatment
- Hair restoration
- Sexual health services
- Bone health management
- Facial rejuvenation with toxins, fillers, and lasers
- Supplements

A well-structured menopause care program could generate significant revenue per patient annually, with the potential for multi-year relationships as women navigate this life stage.

WOMEN AS HEALTHCARE DECISION-MAKERS

Focusing on women's health, particularly menopause care, offers an additional advantage: women are often the primary healthcare decision-makers for their families. Because women make approximately 80% of healthcare decisions in the United States, by establishing trust and providing excellent care to women, practitioners can indirectly influence the healthcare choices of entire families. This trust opens doors to expand services to male partners and other family members, further increasing the practice's patient base and revenue potential.

CASH-BASED SERVICES FOR MENOPAUSE CARE

A menopause-focused practice can offer a wide range of cash-based services, addressing various aspects of women's health during this transition. These may include:

- Comprehensive menopause evaluations
- Hormone therapy (systemic and local)
- Non-hormonal treatments for symptom management
- Vaginal rejuvenation procedures
- Sexual health counseling and treatments
- Bone density screenings and osteoporosis prevention
- Cardiovascular risk assessments
- Weight management and nutrition counseling
- Cognitive function support
- Pelvic floor therapy
- Mindfulness and stress reduction programs
- Sleep disorder evaluations and treatments
- Bioidentical hormone pellet therapy
- Genetic testing for personalized treatment plans
- Menopause-specific and age-related skincare treatments

These services can be bundled into comprehensive care packages, offering women holistic support throughout their menopause journey.

POSITIONING YOUR PRACTICE IN WOMEN'S HEALTH AND MENOPAUSE

Branding your medical practice as a "menopause provider" offers a significant competitive advantage in today's healthcare landscape. This positioning strategy sets your practice apart in a market where specialized menopause care is still relatively uncommon despite the growing demand.

Unique Market Position

By focusing on menopause care, you differentiate your practice from general practitioners, OB/GYNs, and even other functional healthcare providers who offer the same services but don't specifically position themselves or their practice to be focused on menopause. This specialization allows you to:

- Attract a specific, underserved patient demographic

- Be immediately identified as a qualified source of relief for menopausal women

- Reduce direct competition with general practices

- Establish yourself as an expert in a niche field

Expanded Service Offering

Interestingly, a menopause-focused practice can offer many of the same services as other medical practices, but with a specialized lens:

- Hormone therapy becomes "menopause hormone therapy"

- General wellness checks become "menopause wellness assessments"

- Sexual health services are tailored to "menopausal sexual health"

This reframing of services under the menopause umbrella can make your practice more appealing to women seeking specialized care during this life stage.

BUILDING TRUST AND LOYALTY

Women often feel dismissed or misunderstood when seeking help for menopause symptoms. By positioning your practice as menopause-focused, you signal to potential patients that you understand their unique needs. This can lead to:

- Increased patient trust and loyalty
- Higher patient satisfaction rates
- More word-of-mouth referrals

JOINING MENOPAUSE ORGANIZATIONS AND ADVISORY BOARDS

Actively participating in menopause-focused organizations can significantly enhance your practice's reputation and reach. Consider the following strategies:

Benefits of Joining The Menopause Association

The Menopause Association offers several advantages for healthcare professionals:

- Access to a centralized platform with a growing database of articles, interviews, and video content on menopause-related topics

- Opportunities to connect with a network of qualified medical practitioners, professionals, device manufacturers, and product providers

- Potential to contribute to the association's educational resources, enhancing your professional profile

- Alignment with an organization committed to empowering women through education and informed decision-making

- Participation in efforts to address the gap in menopause care, given that only 20% of OB/GYN U.S. residency programs offer training in this area

CREATING ONLINE CONTENT

As a member of The Menopause Association, you can contribute to their growing database of resources:

- Produce articles, interviews, or video content on menopause-related topics

- Share your expertise to help educate women about menopause symptoms and potential treatments

- Engage with patients and other professionals through the association's platform

By consistently producing high-quality, informative content, you position yourself as a thought leader in the field of menopause care while supporting the association's mission to inform and empower women.

NETWORKING AND COLLABORATION

Membership in The Menopause Association provides opportunities to:

- Connect with other menopause specialists and experts in the field

- Collaborate with device manufacturers and product providers in the menopause care space

- Participate in a community dedicated to improving menopause care and women's health

By joining The Menopause Association, you not only enhance your professional development but also contribute to a larger mission of supporting women through the menopause transition, addressing an underserved market, and potentially transforming the landscape of menopause care.

PARTICIPATING AS AN ADVISORY BOARD MEMBER

As a proactive thought leader in the area of menopausal treatment, seek out the opportunity to join The Menopause Association's advisory board. This can:

- Elevate your professional status

- Provide opportunities to shape industry standards and practices

- Offer exposure to potential patients and referral sources

- Further position yourself as a nationally recognized expert in women's health

CREATING ONLINE CONTENT

Develop a strong online presence focused on menopause education:

- Start a blog or podcast discussing menopause-related topics

- Produce educational videos explaining common menopause symptoms and treatments

- Engage with patients and other professionals on social media platforms

By consistently producing high-quality, informative content, you position yourself as a thought leader in the field of menopause care.

EXPANDING INTO AESTHETIC TREATMENTS

Once you've established a strong foundation in menopause care, there's a natural opportunity to expand into aesthetic treatments. Many women seeking menopause care are also interested in addressing age-related cosmetic concerns. By focusing first on a woman's most pressing issues, relief from menopausal conditions, you build a relationship early in their "buying cycle" of other age-related treatments. This is an important strategy for acquiring new clients and sparking exponential growth in your practice.

COMPLEMENTARY AESTHETIC SERVICES

If you don't already, consider offering the following treatments:

- Neurotoxins (Botox, Xeomin) for wrinkle reduction

- Dermal fillers for volume restoration

- Laser treatments for skin rejuvenation

- PRP treatments for hair restoration and sexual health

HOLISTIC APPROACH TO MENOPAUSE CARE

By combining menopause management with aesthetic treatments, you offer patients a comprehensive approach to aging well. This can include:

- Addressing both internal (hormonal) and external (cosmetic) aspects of aging

- Providing a one-stop solution for menopausal women's health and beauty needs

- Increasing patient satisfaction by meeting multiple needs in one practice

INCREASED REVENUE STREAMS

Adding aesthetic services can significantly boost your practice's revenue:

- Most aesthetic treatments are cash-pay, improving profit margins

- Patients seeking menopause care may be more likely to trust you for aesthetic treatments

- Regular aesthetic treatments can increase patient retention and visit frequency

A CALL TO ACTION FOR MEDICAL PROFESSIONALS

The menopause care market represents a significant opportunity for medical professionals seeking to establish or expand their cash-based practices. With millions of women underserved by the current healthcare system, there is a pressing need for specialized, comprehensive care during this critical life stage.

Keep in mind that it's not only about menopause ... it's about aging. Menopause is the differentiator that positions you at the front end of a very long and lucrative buying cycle for women who want to feel better, look better, and live better as they reach this pivotal stage of their lives.

By focusing on menopause, practitioners can:

- Tap into a vast and growing market

- Provide much-needed support to an underserved population

- Develop long-term relationships with patients

- Create substantial revenue streams through comprehensive care packages

- Indirectly influence the healthcare decisions of families, friends, and co-workers

- Differentiate their practice in a competitive healthcare landscape

- Establish themselves as experts in a specialized field

- Expand into complementary services like aesthetic treatments

Now is the moment for visionary practitioners to step into this space, offering the personalized, high-quality care that menopausal women desperately need and deserve. By doing so, they not only stand to build thriving practices but also to make a significant impact on women's health and well-being.

As you consider your practice's future direction, ask yourself: Are you ready to meet the needs of this vast, underserved market? The opportunity to transform women's health and your practice awaits.

What's Ahead: Next, we'll uncover the fundamental drivers of practice growth to turn this opportunity into reality.

CHAPTER 2

FUNDAMENTALS OF BUSINESS GROWTH

WHY IT'S IMPORTANT TO UNDERSTAND WHAT DRIVES THE GROWTH IN YOUR PRACTICE

There are only three ways to grow any business at the most basic level. These principles, introduced to me over two decades ago by legendary marketer Jay Abraham, are particularly relevant for a cash-based medical practice. Let's explore each of these mechanisms:

1. Acquire More Clients

The first method to grow your practice is to increase the number of patients or clients you serve. Too many practitioners fixate solely on this aspect of growth. They spend inordinate amounts of time, energy, and money on acquiring new clients while ignoring the other two elements. Attracting new clients usually involves:

- **Targeted Marketing**: Marketing campaigns that specifically address the needs of your local audience's needs and the treatments and services you provide. Highlight the perceived unique benefits of your cash-based practice.

- **Referral Programs:** Implementation of one or more robust referral systems that encourage satisfied patients to refer their friends and family members who may be experiencing similar issues.

- **Community Outreach:** Organize educational seminars or workshops to help position you as an expert in the field.

- **Online Presence:** Develop a strong online presence through a professional website and active social media accounts. Share valuable content to attract and engage potential patients

2. Increase the Average Purchase Value

The second mechanism for business growth is to increase the amount each patient spends per visit or treatment course:

- **Comprehensive Treatment Plans:** Offer holistic treatment packages that address multiple aspects of menopausal health, such as hormone therapy, weight management, and aesthetics.

- **Premium Services:** Introduce high-value services such as personalized genetic testing or advanced diagnostic procedures that can justify higher fees. Beyond packages, premium services like these elevate the patient experience while boosting revenue.

- **Product Sales:** Offer high-quality supplements, skincare products, or other items specifically designed for menopausal women. This not only increases revenue but also enhances the overall patient experience.

- **Tiered Pricing:** Implement a tiered pricing structure for different levels of care or membership, allowing patients to choose more comprehensive (and higher-priced) options.

3. Increase the Frequency of Purchase

The third driver of growth encouraging patients to visit more often or engage with your practice more frequently:

- **Ongoing Care Programs**: Develop long-term care programs that require regular check-ins and follow-ups. This could include hormone monitoring, weight management, regular skincare treatment, or preventive health screenings.

- **Subscription Models**: Consider implementing a subscription-based model for ongoing care, which ensures regular patient engagement and a steady revenue stream.

- **Patient Education**: Educate patients about the importance of regular check-ups and preventive care during the aging process. This encourages more frequent visits.

- **Diversified Services**: Offer a range of complementary services such as nutrition counseling, hair restoration, Platelet-Rich Plasma injections, treatment for sexual dysfunction, or laser treatments. This gives patients more reasons to engage with your practice regularly.

- **Follow-up Systems**: Implement a robust follow-up system using email, text messages, or a patient portal to remind patients of appointments, share health tips, and maintain ongoing communication.

* * *

Small improvements in any of the three key areas ... acquiring more clients, increasing the average purchase value, and boosting the frequency of purchases ... will have a significant impact on the growth of your cash-based medical practice. Let me show you what I mean:

- Number of Clients = 1200
- Average Spend Per Client Per Visit = $500
- Frequency of Visits Per Year Per Client = 2.

With these basic numbers, the annual revenue from this client base is $1,200,000.

Let's assume you can increase the client base by 10%. Doing so will increase your client base to 1320 and your annual revenue to $1,320,000. An increase in any of the three mechanisms has the same effect ... a 10% increase in one area will result in a 10% increase in total revenue. The growth is linear.

However, you can achieve geometric growth by improving all three areas. For example, let's assume a 10% increase in each of the three mechanisms:

- Number of Clients = 1320

- Average Spend Per Client Per Visit = $550

- Frequency of Visits Per Year Per Client = 2.2. Your revenue jumps to $1,597,200 ... a $397,200 gain, over 33% growth ... not simply 10%.

This is why it is so important to concentrate on improving all three growth mechanisms. Remember, the key is to provide exceptional value at every patient interaction, ensuring that your growth strategies align with delivering high-quality, patient-centered care.

THE SIX STEPS TO BUILDING A SUCCESSFUL MENOPAUSE TREATMENT PRACTICE

To harness these pillars, craft a growth strategy that guides patients from awareness to advocacy, incorporating the three fundamentals of business growth while understanding the patient journey from initial awareness to post-treatment referrals. Each step of this journey requires a targeted approach to effectively attract, engage, and retain patients. It is important to remember that every person interacting with your practice is on one of the following steps and to interact with them differently depending on where they are in their journey.

Following is a detailed explanation covering the six steps:

1. Building Brand Awareness

2. Becoming the Brand of Choice

3. Creating Traffic

4. Converting Consultations

5. Increased Sales Through Expanding Treatment Plans

6. Increase Word-of-Mouth Referrals From Current Clients, Referral Partners, and Strategic Alliances

1. Building Brand Awareness

Importance: Brand awareness is the first step in attracting new patients. It's crucial for establishing a presence in a competitive market and ensuring that potential patients first know you exist.

Strategy: Utilize digital and traditional marketing channels to introduce your practice to potential patients.

Elements:

- **Online Presence:** Website, social media platforms, and SEO (Search Engine Optimization)

- **Content Marketing:** Blog posts, e-books, and educational videos about menopause and treatment options

- **Traditional Advertising:** Local magazines, radio spots, and community events

Methods for Improvement:

- **SEO Optimization**: Ensure your website is optimized for search engines to increase visibility.

- **Social Media Engagement**: Regularly post engaging content and interact with followers to build a community.

- **Collaborations and Sponsorships**: Partner with local women's health organizations and influencers to reach a wider audience.

2. Becoming the Brand of Choice

Importance: This step moves potential patients from simply knowing about your practice to preferring it over competitors due to perceived value and quality.

Strategy: Position your practice as the premier choice through quality services, expert staff, and exceptional patient experiences. Set yourself apart further by establishing yourself as an expert in women's health, specifically in treating menopausal symptoms and conditions.

Elements:

- **Unique Selling Proposition (USP)**: Clearly communicate what sets your practice apart, emphasizing a focus on menopausal care.

- **Patient Reviews and Testimonials**: Showcase positive experiences to build trust.

- **Expert Credentials**: Highlight the qualifications and expertise of you and your medical staff.

Methods for Improvement:

- **Quality Assurance**: Implement strict quality control for treatments and patient care.

- **Patient Education**: Educate patients on the benefits and uniqueness of your menopause treatments.

- **Awards and Certifications**: Pursue industry recognition to establish authority and credibility.

3. Creating Traffic

Importance: Increasing traffic is essential for converting awareness and preference into actual engagement and inquiries. Without interested prospects, you'll struggle to grow.

Strategy: Drive potential patients to your website, social media, or physical location through targeted campaigns.

Elements:

- **Online Advertising**: Use Pay-Per-Click (PPC) and social media ads targeted at women in the relevant age group.

- **Email Marketing**: Send newsletters and informational content to your mailing list.

- **Events and Seminars**: Host educational events to attract visitors to your location.

Methods for Improvement:

- **Targeted Campaigns**: Use data analytics to tailor your advertising efforts to the most likely patients.

- **Opt-in Offers**: Provide value through free information or consultations in exchange for contact details.

- **Local and Organic SEO**: Optimize for local search queries to attract nearby patients.

4. Converting Consultations

Importance: Conversion is critical for turning interest into revenue. High traffic means little without a strong conversion rate

Strategy: Turn inquiries and visits into booked appointments and treatments through effective communication and patient care

Elements:

- **Staff Training**: Equip your staff with the skills to effectively communicate treatment options.

- **Online Booking**: Make it easy for patients to book appointments online.

- **Special Offers**: Limited-time promotions to incentivize immediate bookings.

Methods for Improvement:

- **Follow-up Strategies**: Implement a system for following up on inquiries using an automated CRM (Customer Relationship Management) system such as High Level.

- **Conversion Rate Optimization (CRO)**: Use analytics to refine the booking process on your website.

- **Patient Feedback**: Use patient feedback to improve the consultation process and address any concerns.

5. Increased Sales Through Expanding Treatment Plans

Importance: Maximizing value from each patient enhances overall practice success without necessarily increasing patient base.

Strategy: Increase the average treatment value through comprehensive care plans and promoting holistic approaches. Always offer patients upsells and cross-sells, ensuring they receive the best possible outcomes.

Elements:

- **Comprehensive Care Plans**: Offer long-term treatment packages for menopause management.

- **Wellness Programs**: Encourage ongoing care with holistic health programs.

- **Complementary Treatments**: Offer additional services that support menopause treatment.

Methods for Improvement:

- **Staff Education**: Provide ongoing training for staff on the latest menopause treatments and patient care.

- **Personalized Recommendations**: Use patient data to make tailored suggestions for additional treatments or services.

- **Patient Education**: Educate patients on the benefits of comprehensive menopause management.

6. Increase Word-of-Mouth Referrals From Current Clients, Referral Partners, and Strategic Alliances

Importance: Referrals and word-of-mouth are highly effective and cost-efficient ways to attract new patients who will likely trust recommendations from people they know.

Strategy: Encourage satisfied patients to refer friends and family, and share their positive experiences. Build relationships with other non-competitive business owners who share the audience, such as hair salons, personal trainers, and boutiques.

Elements:

- **Referral Programs:** Offer incentives for patients who refer new patients.

- **Social Proof:** Encourage patients to share their experiences on social media.

- **Community Engagement:** Participate in local women's health events and charities to build goodwill.

Methods for Improvement:

- **Incentivize Referrals:** Offer discounts or additional services for both the referrer and the referred.

- **Patient Appreciation Events:** Host exclusive events for loyal patients to encourage sharing their experiences.

- **Social Media Engagement:** Actively engage with patients who mention your practice online to amplify their messages.

* * *

Implementing this comprehensive strategy requires careful planning, consistent execution, and regular evaluation to adapt to changing market conditions and patient needs. By methodically addressing each step of the patient journey, a menopause treatment practice can build a strong brand, attract and retain patients, and achieve sustained growth. Let's dig a little deeper into each phase of your practice growth.

STEP ONE: BUILDING BRAND AWARENESS

Digital Marketing

Online Presence:

Website: Develop a professional, user-friendly website that showcases your services, staff expertise, and client testimonials. Ensure it's optimized for SEO (Search Engine Optimization) with relevant keywords to improve visibility on search engine results pages (SERPs).

Social Media Platforms: Utilize platforms like Instagram, Facebook, and LinkedIn to share engaging content, including before-and-after photos, client testimonials, short videos on treatments, and educational posts about menopause, graceful aging, wellness, and beauty. Regular interaction and timely responses to comments and messages are crucial.

SEO: Implement a robust SEO strategy focusing on local keywords ("menopause treatment near me", "[Your City] hormone therapy") and other services offered. Blog posts addressing common questions or concerns related to your services can also improve organic search visibility.

Content Marketing: Create valuable content that positions you and your practice as a thought leader in the industry. This can include blog posts on menopause, hormone replacement therapy, skincare routines, the benefits of certain treatments, and wellness tips. Videos and live sessions showcasing treatments, Q&A sessions with experts, and behind-the-scenes looks at your practice can significantly enhance engagement.

Traditional Advertising

Local Magazines and Radio Spots: Advertise in local lifestyle magazines and on radio stations to reach a broader audience. Tailor your messaging to highlight the unique benefits of choosing your practice, such as exclusive treatments for menopause, expert staff, or a serene environment.

Community Events: Participate in or sponsor local events, health fairs, and charity functions to increase your visibility within the community. This not only introduces your brand to potential clients but also establishes your practice as a community-oriented business.

Collaborations and Sponsorships

Influencer Partnerships: Partner with local influencers and wellness bloggers for sponsored content or social media takeovers. Choose partners whose followers align with your target demographic to ensure relevance and engagement.

Local Business Collaborations: Collaborate with complementary businesses such as gyms, yoga studios, hair salons, boutiques, and health food stores to offer joint promotions or events. This can introduce your practice to clients who are already interested in health and wellness.

Additional Strategies

Email Marketing: Build an email list through your website and in-office promotions. Send regular newsletters that provide value through health tips, longevity news, and exclusive offers. Personalization and segmentation can increase the relevance and effectiveness of your campaigns.

Client Reviews and Testimonials: Encourage satisfied clients to leave reviews on Google, Yelp, and social media. Positive reviews can significantly influence potential clients' perceptions and decisions. Feature these testimonials prominently on your website and social media channels.

Consistency in Branding: Ensure consistency in your branding across all platforms, including logo, color scheme, messaging, and tone. Consistent branding helps increase recognition and reinforces your professional image.

* * *

Building brand awareness is an ongoing process that requires creativity, consistency, and engagement with your target audience. By effectively implementing these strategies, your medical practice can increase its visibility, attract new clients, and build a solid foundation for growth and success.

STEP TWO: BECOMING THE BRAND OF CHOICE

Unique Selling Proposition (USP)

Clearly Define and Communicate Your USP: Identify what makes your practice unique compared to competitors. In addition to a focus on menopause, this could include exclusive treatments, advanced technology, superior expertise, or a unique approach to client care. Communicate this USP across all marketing channels, including your website, social media, advertising, and in-office branding. Make sure your USP resonates with your target audience's needs and desires.

Customer Reviews and Testimonials

Leverage Positive Experiences: Actively encourage happy clients to share their experiences online. This can include direct requests following a service, offering incentives for reviews, or creating easy-to-share social media posts. Highlight these testimonials on your website, in marketing materials, and on social media. Video testimonials can be particularly impactful.

Expert Credentials

Showcase Staff Expertise: Create detailed profiles for your staff, highlighting their qualifications, experience, and areas of specialization. Share these profiles on your website and social media channels. Host events, workshops, or webinars where your experts can share their knowledge and interact with potential clients, further establishing their authority and your brand's credibility.

Quality Assurance

Implement High Standards: Ensure that every aspect of your service, from initial consultation to post-treatment care, meets high standards. Regularly train staff on best practices and customer service excellence. Solicit feedback from clients to identify areas for improvement and act on this feedback to continuously enhance service quality.

Client Education

Inform and Educate Your Clients: Develop educational content that helps clients understand the benefits and processes of your treatments. This can include blog posts, videos, FAQs, and informational brochures. Use layman's terms to explain complex procedures, focusing on benefits and safety to reassure potential clients.

Awards and Certifications

Pursue Recognition: Apply for industry awards and certifications that can bolster your reputation. Display these accolades prominently in your office, treatment rooms, and marketing materials. Share any nominations, awards, association memberships, or recognitions in press releases, on your website, and across social media platforms to build trust and prestige.

Personalization and Experience

Offer Personalized Experiences: Use client consultations to tailor recommendations and treatments to individual needs, enhancing satisfaction and perceived value. Implement a client management system to track preferences, past treatments, and feedback, allowing for personalized communication and offers.

Aftercare and Follow-Up

Extend the Customer Relationship Beyond the Visit: Provide comprehensive aftercare instructions and support, including follow-up calls or messages to check on client satisfaction and address any concerns. This level of care not only improves the overall experience but also encourages clients to return and recommend your spa to others.

* * *

By focusing on these strategies, your practice can transition from being just another option to becoming the preferred choice for clients. Emphasizing unique offerings, quality, expertise, and personalized experiences cultivates a loyal client base that views your practice as the go-to destination for their menopause wellness and aesthetic needs.

STEP THREE: CREATING TRAFFIC

Online Advertising

Leverage Targeted Digital Campaigns: Utilize pay-per-click (PPC ... Pay-Per-Click) advertising on search engines with keywords specific to your services and location. Tailor your ad copy to address the needs and interests of your target audience.

Run targeted social media ads on platforms where your potential clients are most active. Use demographic, geographic, and behavioral targeting to reach individuals likely interested in your services.

Email Marketing

Engage and Nurture Leads: Build an email list through website sign-ups, in-office promotions, and social media calls-to-action. Offer a valuable incentive for signing up, such as a discount on their first visit or a free consultation.

Send regular, value-packed emails that include exclusive offers, informative content about treatments, and personal success stories. Segment your email list to tailor messages to different audience needs and interests, improving engagement and driving traffic.

Events and Open Houses

Host Engaging In-Person and Virtual Events: Organize open houses, treatment demonstrations, wellness seminars, and Q&A sessions with your experts. These events can attract new visitors to your practice and provide an opportunity for direct engagement.

Consider virtual events or webinars to reach a broader audience. These can be particularly effective for engaging potential clients who are interested in your services but haven't visited your practice.

Content Marketing

Provide Valuable, Shareable Content: Create informative and engaging content that addresses common questions, concerns, and interests related to your services. This can include blog posts, videos, infographics, and podcasts.

Optimize content for SEO (Search Engine Optimization) to improve visibility in search engine results. Use social media to share your content widely, encouraging shares and interactions to increase reach.

Local SEO

Optimize for Local Searches: Ensure your business is listed on Google My Business and other relevant online directories. Keep your listings updated with accurate information, including your address, phone number, and hours of operation.

Encourage clients to leave reviews on your Google My Business listing. Positive reviews can improve your visibility in local search results and attract more traffic.

Collaborations and Partnerships

Leverage Local Networks: Partner with other local businesses, such as fitness centers, wellness clinics, and beauty salons, for cross-promotion. You can offer mutual discounts, co-host events, or share each other's marketing materials.

Collaborate with local influencers and bloggers in the health and wellness space. They can help promote your spa to their followers through sponsored content, reviews, or social media mentions.

Referral Programs

Encourage Word-of-Mouth: Implement a referral program that rewards existing clients for bringing in new customers. Offer incentives that are appealing and relevant, such as discounts on future services, free products, or exclusive access to new treatments.

Make it easy for clients to refer others by providing them with referral cards or a simple online referral system.

* * *

By implementing these strategies, you can significantly increase traffic to your practice, both online and offline. The key is to use a mix of digital and traditional marketing techniques tailored to your target audience's preferences and behaviors. Engaging potential clients through multiple touchpoints can effectively draw them into your practice, setting the stage for conversion and long-term loyalty.

STEP FOUR: CONVERTING CONSULTATIONS

Sales Training

Equip Your Team with the Right Skills: Provide comprehensive sales training for your staff, focusing on consultative selling techniques. This approach involves understanding the client's needs and recommending services that best address those needs rather than pushing for the most expensive options.

Role-play different customer scenarios in training sessions to prepare staff for handling objections, answering questions, and closing sales effectively.

Realize that every person on your team is in "sales." Every touchpoint, every interaction, and every conversation can have an impact on your revenue.

Embrace the position that you would be doing your client a disservice if you did not offer them each and every treatment option that would help them feel better, look better, and improve their overall quality of life. Look for every opportunity to offer additional services.

Online Booking System

Streamline the Booking Process: Implement an fast, intuitive online booking system on your website and social media platforms. Ensure it's mobile-friendly, as many clients will book appointments from their phones.

The booking system should allow clients to see available times, select services, and even choose their preferred provider. Confirmation and reminder emails or text messages can reduce no-shows and enhance the customer experience.

Special Offers and Incentives

Create Urgency and Value: Limited-time offers can create a sense of urgency, encouraging clients to book sooner rather than later. These can include discounts on services, package deals, or add-ons at a reduced price.

Consider offering a first-time client discount or a complimentary consultation to lower the barrier to booking.

Follow-up Strategies

Maximize Every Inquiry: Develop a follow-up process for inquiries that don't immediately convert. This could involve a sequence of emails, texts, or calls to provide additional information, answer questions, and encourage booking.

Personalize follow-up communications based on the potential client's expressed interests or concerns to make them more effective.

Conversion Rate Optimization (CRO)

Refine Your Online Experience: Regularly analyze the performance of your website and booking system. Look for areas where visitors drop off without booking and test changes to layout, content, or the booking process to improve conversions. CRO (Conversion Rate Optimization) helps refine this process using analytics.

User feedback can be invaluable in identifying obstacles to conversion. Consider using surveys or feedback forms to gather insights from users who exit without booking.

Client Feedback

Learn and Adapt from Client Interactions: Encourage feedback from clients about their booking experience and overall satisfaction with your services. This feedback can highlight areas for improvement in your sales process.

Implement changes based on client feedback to continuously enhance the booking experience and conversion rates.

Monitoring and Analytics

Track Your Success and Adjust Accordingly: Use analytics tools to track conversions from different channels (e.g., website, social media, email marketing). Understand which channels are most effective at driving bookings and allocate your marketing budget accordingly.

Monitor key performance indicators (KPIs ... Key Performance Indicators) such as conversion rate, average transaction value, and customer acquisition cost to evaluate the effectiveness of your sales strategies and make data-driven decisions.

* * *

By focusing on these areas, your practice can effectively convert interest into bookings and sales, maximizing the return on your marketing investment. The goal is to make the process as seamless and inviting as possible, encouraging clients to take the final step in their customer journey with your practice.

STEP FIVE: ADDING MORE SALES

Package Deals

Offer Attractive Packages: Create packages that bundle popular treatments together at a slightly reduced price. These could cater to specific client needs, such as anti-aging and ongoing menopause treatment.

Highlight the benefits and savings of purchasing packages over individual treatments. Make sure these packages are prominently displayed on your website, in office marketing materials, and discussed during client consultations.

Membership Programs

Encourage Repeat Business: Develop a membership program that offers value beyond discounts, such as priority booking, a free monthly treatment, or exclusive access to new services. Memberships encourage clients to return more frequently and commit to your practice long-term.

Use memberships to smooth out revenue fluctuations and build a steady base of loyal clients.

Product Sales

Integrate Retail into Client Experience: Offer a selection of skincare products, supplements, or in-home devices that complement your services. Train staff to recommend products based on the treatments clients receive, turning each service into an opportunity to address home care needs.

Display products attractively in your office and feature them on your website. Consider offering product demonstrations or samples to encourage purchases.

Staff Incentives

Motivate Your Team to Upsell and Cross-Sell: Implement a reward system for staff who successfully upsell or cross-sell services and products. Incentives could include bonuses, commissions, or non-monetary rewards like extra time off.

Regularly train staff on the features and benefits of your services and products, ensuring they can confidently recommend add-ons that enhance the client's experience.

Personalized Recommendations

Leverage Client Data for Tailored Suggestions: Use client consultations and history to make personalized service and product recommendations. A client who frequently books hormone replacement therapy treatments might be interested in a package that includes laser vaginal rejuvenation, The O-Shot Procedure, hair restoration, and related products.

Implementing a CRM (Customer Relationship Management) system can help track client preferences and treatment history, enabling more effective personalized marketing.

Client Education

Inform Clients About Benefits: Educate clients on the benefits of additional treatments and products during their visit and through your marketing channels. This can include blog posts, email newsletters, and social media content that provides valuable information on laser treatments for skincare, wellness, and the benefits of regular treatments.

Hosting educational events or workshops in your office can also engage clients and introduce them to services or products they haven't tried yet.

Monitoring and Feedback

Track Performance and Solicit Client Input: Monitor the performance of upselling and cross-selling initiatives to identify what works best. This can help refine your approach and focus on the most effective strategies.

Ask for client feedback on their experiences with packages, memberships, and product purchases. This feedback can provide insights into client preferences and potential areas for improvement or expansion.

* * *

By focusing on these strategies, your medical practice can not only increase the average transaction value per client but also enhance client satisfaction by offering comprehensive care and value-added services.

Effective communication, personalized recommendations, and staff motivation are key to successfully adding more sales while maintaining a high level of client care and satisfaction.

STEP SIX: GENERATING REFERRAL AND WORD OF MOUTH CLIENTS

Referral Programs

Create Compelling Referral Programs: Develop referral programs that reward both the referrer and the new client. Rewards could include discounts on future services, complimentary treatments, or spa products. Make sure the incentives are enticing enough to motivate clients to participate.

Communicate the details of your referral program through all touchpoints: in-office signage, email newsletters, social media, and during appointments. Training your staff to mention the program during client interactions can also boost participation.

Social Proof

Encourage Social Sharing and Reviews: Ask satisfied clients to share their experiences on social media, tagging your practice's profile and using any branded hashtags you've created. You might consider creating a photo-friendly spot within your spa specifically for clients to take and share pictures.

Make it easy for clients to leave reviews by sending follow-up emails with links to your Google Business profile, Yelp, or other relevant review platforms. Display placards in your treatment rooms and at the checkout desk with a notice for clients to post a review online. Include a QR code that can be scanned, sending the client directly to your profile. Positive online reviews serve as powerful social proof for potential clients researching your practice.

Community Engagement

Build a Positive Local Presence: Participate in local events, charities, and community initiatives. This not only helps to build brand awareness but also establishes your office as a community-minded business, encouraging word-of-mouth referrals.

Hosting free workshops or seminars on menopause, skincare, and wellness can also position your practice as a trusted local authority, further encouraging referrals.

Incentivize Referrals

Make Referring Easy and Rewarding: Provide clients with easy-to-share referral cards or a simple digital referral system that allows them to refer friends and family via email or social media.

Regularly remind your clients of the referral program through various channels and highlight the benefits they and their friends can enjoy. This keeps the program top of mind and encourages ongoing participation.

Client Appreciation Events

Host Exclusive Events for Loyal Clients: Organize special events, such as VIP nights, appreciation dinners, or exclusive previews of new treatments, for your most loyal clients and encourage them to bring a friend. These events can make clients feel valued and more likely to speak positively about your spa. Use these events as an opportunity to gather feedback, further personalize your services, and strengthen relationships with your clients.

Social Media Engagement

Leverage Social Media to Amplify Messages: Actively engage with clients who mention your practice on social media by liking, commenting, and sharing their posts. This not only shows appreciation but also increases the visibility of their positive messages to a broader audience.

Create shareable content that clients are likely to want to post on their own social media profiles, such as educational posts, behind-the-scenes looks, or special promotions.

Implementing a Feedback Loop

Use Feedback to Enhance the Referral Process: Solicit feedback from both new clients who were referred and the clients who made the referrals to understand what's working and what could be improved in your referral program.

Use this feedback to make continuous improvements, ensuring that the referral process remains attractive and beneficial for all parties involved.

* * *

By focusing on these strategies, your practice can turn satisfied clients into powerful advocates, helping to attract a steady stream of new clients through referrals and word-of-mouth. This approach not only reduces marketing costs but also builds a strong, loyal client base rooted in trust and positive experiences.

DEVELOPING YOUR GROWTH PLAN

Implementing this comprehensive strategy requires careful planning, consistent execution, and regular evaluation to adapt to changing market conditions and patient needs. By methodically addressing each step of the patient journey, a menopause treatment practice can build a strong brand, attract and retain patients, and achieve sustained growth. In the next chapter, I'll address how to begin building your growth plan.

What's Ahead: Next, we'll evaluate your practice to ensure every effort counts toward sustainable growth.

CHAPTER 3

EVALUATING YOUR PRACTICE SO YOU NEVER WASTE MONEY ON INEFFECTIVE PROGRAMS AGAIN

In the previous chapter, we identified the three ways to grow any business and the six steps for predictable growth. Just as you'd care for a patient, assess your practice with:

- Examination and assessment ...

- Diagnosis and treatment plan ...

- Implementation and monitoring ...

BUSINESS GROWTH

Acquiring New Clients

Ask yourself these questions:

- How does your practice rate at generating a steady stream of new prospects/clients?

- How well is your marketing team delivering here?

We'll talk about client retention in an upcoming chapter, but don't overlook that selling to an existing client is easier and more cost-effective than acquiring a new client. When investing in client acquisition, spend as much time, effort, and money to maintain that client. Acquiring clients and keeping clients is where real business growth occurs.

In the client acquisition phase, to achieve geometric business growth, don't target individuals who are only looking for the cheapest cost. They are likely to be a "one and done" client who jumps from provider to provider, without any true loyalty except to the price. It's a vicious cycle, and you'll burn out trying to convert prospects continually.

Are you tracking KPIs (Key Performance Indicators) such as:

- Leads
- Visits
- Conversion Rate (from ads to interest, from interest to booking an appointment, from booking an appointment to showing up for the phone or in-person appointment, to closing the prospect and generating revenue)
- COA (Cost of Acquisition) ... how much does it cost to acquire a new client?
- ROAS (Return on Ad Spend) ... how much revenue do you generate compared to ad spend?

Give your practice a score from 1 to 100.

Average Revenue Per Visit

Ask yourself these questions:

- What are we doing to maximize each client's average spend per visit?
- Are we upselling and cross-selling consistently?

- Do you or some of your other providers consistently perform better than others?

- Do you have specific plans to help your team upsell and cross-sell?

- Do you have training and scripts to help you and your staff identify and capitalize on all opportunities?

It is your moral and ethical responsibility to offer your clients anything and everything they may need to improve their condition and reach their goals. Shift your mindset from "selling" to "helping." Develop personalized treatment plans that can be administered over time. Create custom packages that can be offered at a discount price when bundled together. This not only increases the average revenue per visit but also boosts the frequency of purchase.

Give your practice a score from 1 to 100.

FREQUENCY OF PURCHASE

Do you follow up with clients to ensure they stay on their intended schedule for regular treatments? For example, missed follow-ups can slash revenue by 25% on hormone replacement patients if you allow them to postpone their quarterly visit by one month each quarter. Skipping one month equates to only three visits per year instead of four. The same can be said for your aesthetic clients ... Make sure they visit every quarter for Botox or Xeomin treatments by incorporating a robust appointment reminder system.

You can encourage clients to visit more frequently by contacting them by email, text, or phone when you are offering a new treatment or running a special promotion. You can also run a VIP promotion, not broadcast to the masses. Limit it to your special clients and personally invite them to participate.

Give your practice a score from 1 to 100.

GRADING AND EVALUATING THE THREE WAYS TO GROW YOUR REVENUE

A score below 70 indicates this is an area in which you need to seek ways to improve immediately. Address these areas with your marketing team and staff. Proactively focusing on continual improvement will profoundly affect your overall profit.

Grading the Six Steps

You must periodically grade yourself for each of the six steps explained in Chapter 2. Assigning an honest score to each step will identify your areas of strength and, most importantly, where you have room for improvement.

Start by evaluating and ranking yourself across the six steps for business growth. Order your proficiency or dominance in each area from best to worst. Assign a number, 1, 2, 3, 4, 5, or 6 for each step. Use each number only one time. When you have your steps ordered, multiply the corresponding score by 5 to get the percentage of "focus" you should apply to each step.

For example:

- **Brand Awareness – 1**: You have done a great job reaching a broad audience in your market area and are well-positioned against other practices. Your practice is very well known in your market area. This is the step you rank as your best.

- **Becoming the Brand of Choice – 2**: You have an excellent reputation. When prospects seek a practice, you are one of the top choices in your market area. This is your second best area.

- **Traffic – 5**: You don't have a consistent flow of new prospects, which results in less-than-optimal sales opportunities. It is definitely an area that needs improvement. It's not your worst, but it needs help. Rank this number 5.

- **Sales – 4:** You or your staff are not converting many new prospects into paying clients. Either the prospects are not well suited for your offerings, or your staff is not as good as they should be in converting prospects to paying clients. Traffic and Sales go hand in hand. There is no point in increasing the traffic if you and your team are not converting those prospects into clients. Let's rank this as 4.

- **Increased Sales – 6:** You seldom upsell or cross-sell your current clients when they come in for treatment. Your average ticket price is relatively low compared to your peers. Clients don't visit as often as they should to maintain optimal results. You and/or your staff are hesitant to introduce additional procedures during appointments, even though you know your client can benefit from the treatment. You know for sure this is a weakness with you and your staff. Rank it in last place, number 6.

- **Referrals and Word of Mouth – 3:** Most of your new clients come from referrals from current clients, referral partners, or strategic alliances. Advertising hasn't been effective for you, so you continue to rely heavily on word-of-mouth referrals. I have a complete section on referrals in an upcoming chapter. It will explain why referrals should be a focus of your practice. If most of your business comes from referrals, it's usually because those prospects are the easiest to convert. For now, you'll rank this as your third-best area of practice. However, in most cases, it ranks high because you're not optimizing Traffic, Sales, and Increasing Sales.

Multiply Your Ranking/Score by 5 to Calculate Your Focus

Now that you've ranked each step, we'll calculate where you should apply your focus for improvement. Multiply each rank by 5 and consider it a percentage of your time. The total of all six steps will be 105%, but it is easier to view and think about if we use round numbers.

- Brand Awareness – 1 x 5% = 5%
- Becoming the Brand of Choice – 2 x 5% = 10%
- Traffic – 5 x 5% = 25%
- Sales – 4 x 5% = 20%
- Increased Sales – 6 x 5% = 30%
- Referrals and Word of Mouth – 3 x 5% = 15%

Reorder The Steps From Lowest to Highest Focus

Now reorder the steps from lowest to highest. Your best, highest functioning, steps will have the lowest percentage. Therefore the lowest rankings steps will require the least amount of time, effort, and finances. Conversely, the highest percentage steps will require the most amount of attention. You'll see that the six steps are ranked in order from 5% to 30%. The top three areas should be the areas you address first. While this may not be a completely accurate representation of your proficiency in each of the six steps, it is a great starting point to identify the most blatant offenders and where you stand to gain the most with a little improvement.

- Brand Awareness – 5%
- Becoming the Brand of Choice – 10%
- Referrals and Word of Mouth – 15%
- Sales – 20%
- Traffic – 25%
- Increased Sales – 30%

Your Lens For Making Business Decisions

With your scores in hand, let's turn evaluation into action. Now that you've scored each of the six steps, you can reflect on your current initiatives to decide if you're applying attention where you need it the most. Evaluate where you invest time, energy, or money and reallocate resources as necessary.

When evaluating a new marketing proposal, strategy, or any new initiative, start by determining which of the six steps it will likely improve. In most cases, a well designed initiative will affect two or sometimes three of the steps.

Plan any new initiatives so the plan delivers the greatest impact and the biggest return in your weakest areas. In other words, work on your weak links first. Improve them to the point that on your next self-evaluation, they move up at least one step in order. Spend your time, energy, and money in the areas where it is needed the most.

For example, develop the Traffic phase so you have an adequate number of sales opportunities. Ideally, your paid or influenced traffic should match or exceed your referral traffic. At the same time or before driving a high volume of traffic, you should also be working on sales training for your staff. If your team is not converting prospects into clients and revenue, then you don't have a Traffic problem. You have a Sales problem. Work on improving your conversions before generating more leads that don't close.

Let's dive into more specific action items to ensure continual improvement.

GRADING EACH OF THE SIX STEPS TO ENSURE CONTINUED GROWTH

Brand Awareness: The Art of Being Known

In the healthcare industry, patients have numerous options when seeking medical care. Building brand awareness ensures that your practice stands out from the competition and remains top-of-mind for potential patients. By increasing visibility and recognition, you create a foundation of trust and credibility that can lead to increased patient acquisition and retention.

For a menopause-focused practice, brand awareness is particularly vital. Many women may be hesitant to seek treatment or may not know where to turn for specialized care. By establishing your practice as a knowledgeable and trustworthy resource, you can bridge this gap and attract patients who might otherwise not seek treatment.

To ensure your brand awareness efforts are effective, it's essential to regularly evaluate and grade your performance. Consider the following metrics:

- **Website Traffic:** Monitor the number of visitors to your website and their engagement levels. Are they spending time on key pages? Are they taking desired actions like booking appointments?

- **Social Media Engagement:** Track follower growth, post engagement rates, and the reach of your content. Are your posts generating discussions and shares?

- **Patient Acquisition:** Keep track of how new patients are finding your practice. Are they mentioning your online content, social media presence, or local advertising?

- **Brand Mentions:** Use tools to monitor mentions of your practice online and in local media. Are you being recognized as a leader in menopause treatment?

An easy way to rank each of the six steps is to grade your performance in each area on a scale of 1-100, with 100 being excellent. If you score below 70, it's time to reassess and improve your strategy.

Continuous Improvement

Brand awareness is not a one-time effort but an ongoing process. Continuously refine your approach based on performance data and patient feedback. Consider these methods for improvement:

- **SEO Optimization**: Regularly update your website content and structure to improve search engine rankings. SEO (Search Engine Optimization) enhances online visibility.

- **Social Media Strategy**: Experiment with different types of content and posting schedules to maximize engagement.

- **Collaborations and Partnerships**: Seek out partnerships with local women's health organizations or influencers to expand your reach.

By prioritizing brand awareness and consistently evaluating your efforts, you can create a strong foundation for your medical practice's growth and success in the competitive field of menopause treatment.

Becoming the Brand of Choice: Elevating Your Medical Practice

Once you've established brand awareness, the next crucial step in growing your medical practice is becoming the brand of choice for potential patients. This transition is particularly important for practices specializing in menopause treatment, where trust and expertise are paramount.

The Importance of Being the Preferred Brand

In the competitive healthcare landscape, simply being known is not enough. To truly thrive, your practice must be the one that patients actively choose over others. This preference stems from a perception of superior value, quality, and expertise. For a menopause-focused practice, becoming the brand of choice means being recognized as the go-to expert for women seeking specialized care during this significant life transition.

Evaluating and Grading Your Performance

To assess how well you're establishing yourself as the brand of choice, consider these metrics:

- **Patient Retention Rate**: A high retention rate indicates satisfaction and preference for your practice.

- **New Patient Referrals**: Satisfied patients who recommend your practice are a strong indicator of brand preference.

- **Online Reviews and Ratings**: Monitor your ratings on healthcare review sites and social media platforms.

- **Appointment Wait Times**: Short wait times for new patient appointments suggest high demand and efficient operations.

- **Treatment Success Rates**: Track and communicate your success rates for various menopause-related treatments.

Grade your performance in this area on a scale of 1-100. Aim for scores of 70 or higher to ensure you're truly becoming the brand of choice in your market area.

CONTINUOUS IMPROVEMENT STRATEGIES

To further solidify your position as the preferred brand for menopause treatment, consider these methods:

- **Implement Rigorous Quality Assurance**: Regularly review and refine your treatment protocols and patient care processes to ensure consistent, high-quality outcomes.

- **Enhance Patient Education:** Develop comprehensive educational materials that explain the uniqueness and benefits of your approach to menopause treatment. This could include articles, brochures, videos, or a dedicated section on your website.

- **Pursue Industry Recognition:** Actively seek out and apply for relevant awards and certifications in women's health and menopause care. Display these accolades prominently in your practice and in your marketing materials.

- **Offer Innovative Services:** Stay at the forefront of menopause treatment by introducing new, evidence-based therapies or holistic approaches that address the full spectrum of menopausal symptoms.

- **Cultivate Partnerships:** Collaborate with other healthcare providers, women's health organizations, and community groups to expand your reach and reinforce your expertise.

By consistently delivering exceptional care, clearly communicating your unique value, and actively working to improve and innovate, you can establish your practice as the undisputed brand of choice for menopause treatment in your area. This position not only attracts new patients but also fosters loyalty among existing ones, creating a strong foundation for sustained growth and success.

CREATING TRAFFIC: DRIVING POTENTIAL PATIENTS TO YOUR PRACTICE

Creating traffic is a crucial step in growing your menopause treatment practice. It bridges the gap between brand awareness and patient acquisition, turning potential patients' interest into tangible engagement with your practice.

The Importance of Creating Traffic

In the competitive healthcare landscape, being known is not enough. Actively driving traffic to your practice's online and physical presence is essential for several reasons:

- **Increased Visibility**: Higher traffic volumes enhance your practice's online and offline visibility, reinforcing your position as a leading menopause treatment provider.

- **Opportunity for Conversion**: More traffic means more opportunities to convert interested individuals into patients, directly impacting your practice's growth.

- **Data Collection**: Increased traffic provides valuable data on patient behavior and preferences, allowing you to refine your marketing strategies and service offerings.

- **Competitive Edge**: Practices that successfully generate high traffic volumes often outperform competitors in patient acquisition and retention.

Strategies for Creating Traffic

To effectively drive traffic to your menopause treatment practice, consider implementing the following strategies:

- **Online Advertising**: Leverage pay-per-click (PPC ... Pay-Per-Click) and social media ads aimed at women in the appropriate age group for menopause treatment.

- **Email Marketing**: Create a strong email marketing campaign to distribute newsletters and informational content about menopause and your treatments to your mailing list.

- **Events and Seminars:** Organize educational events and seminars focused on menopause-related topics to draw visitors to your physical location and demonstrate your expertise.

- **Search Engine Optimization (SEO):** Enhance your website for local search queries to attract nearby patients looking for menopause treatment. SEO (Search Engine Optimization) boosts online discoverability.

- **Content Marketing:** Develop valuable, shareable content that addresses common questions and concerns about menopause, establishing your practice as a reliable resource.

Evaluating and Grading Your Performance

To assess the effectiveness of your traffic generation efforts, consider these key metrics:

- **Website Traffic:** Monitor the number of visitors to your website and their engagement levels. Are they spending time on key pages? Are they taking desired actions like booking appointments?

- **New vs. Returning Visitors:** Track the ratio of new to returning visitors. A healthy mix indicates both growing awareness and patient loyalty.

- **Traffic Sources:** Analyze where your traffic is coming from (e.g., organic search, paid ads, social media, referrals) to understand which channels are most effective.

- **Conversion Rate:** Measure the percentage of visitors who take desired actions, such as booking consultations or signing up for newsletters.

- **Exit Rate:** Monitor at which point visitors leave your website to identify potential areas for improvement in user experience or content.

Grade your performance in this area on a scale of 1-100, with 100 being excellent. If you score below 70, it's time to reassess and improve your strategy for generating traffic.

Continuous Improvement Strategies

To enhance your traffic generation efforts:

- **Targeted Campaigns**: Use data analytics to tailor your advertising efforts to the most likely patients seeking menopause treatment.

- **Opt-in Offers**: Provide value through free information or consultations in exchange for contact details, building your mailing list.

- **Local SEO**: Optimize for local search queries to attract nearby patients specifically looking for menopause treatment options.

- **Content Optimization**: Regularly update and improve your website content to maintain relevance and attract organic traffic.

- **User Experience**: Ensure your website is mobile-friendly and loads quickly to reduce bounce rates and improve engagement.

By focusing on these strategies and consistently evaluating your performance, you can create a steady stream of traffic to your menopause treatment practice, setting the stage for increased patient acquisition and practice growth.

Converting Consultations: Turning Interest into Revenue

Converting consultations into paying clients is a critical step in the growth of your menopause treatment practice. This phase bridges the gap between attracting potential patients and generating revenue, making it essential for the financial health and sustainability of your practice.

The Importance of Conversion

Effective conversion of consultations is crucial for several reasons:

- **Revenue Generation**: Consultations that lead to treatments directly impact your practice's bottom line.

- **Return on Investment**: High conversion rates ensure that your marketing efforts and resources spent on attracting potential clients yield tangible results.

- **Patient Satisfaction**: A smooth conversion process often correlates with higher patient satisfaction, as it indicates that you're meeting their needs effectively.

- **Practice Reputation**: Successfully converting consultations can lead to positive word-of-mouth referrals, further enhancing your practice's growth potential.

Strategies for Effective Conversion

To optimize your consultation-to-client conversion rate, consider implementing the following strategies:

- **Staff Training**: Equip your team with the skills to effectively communicate treatment options and address patient concerns. This includes training on consultative selling techniques and in-depth knowledge of menopause treatments.

- **Streamlined Booking Process**: Implement an easy-to-use online booking system that allows patients to schedule appointments quickly and conveniently.

- **Follow-up System**: Develop a robust follow-up process for inquiries that don't immediately convert, using personalized communication to address specific patient needs and concerns.

- **Special Offers**: Create limited-time promotions or package deals to incentivize immediate bookings.

- **Patient Education**: Provide comprehensive information about your treatments and their benefits during consultations to help patients make informed decisions.

EVALUATING AND GRADING YOUR PERFORMANCE

To assess the effectiveness of your conversion efforts, consider these key metrics:

- **Conversion Rate**: Calculate the percentage of consultations that result in booked treatments or procedures.

- **Average Transaction Value**: Monitor the average amount spent by patients who convert from consultations.

- **Time to Conversion**: Track how long it typically takes from initial consultation to booking a treatment.

- **Patient Feedback**: Collect and analyze feedback from both converted and non-converted consultations to identify areas for improvement.

- **Staff Performance**: Evaluate individual staff members' conversion rates to identify top performers and areas for additional training.

Grade your performance in this area on a scale of 1-100, with 100 being excellent. If you score below 70, it's time to sharpen your sales approach.

CONTINUOUS IMPROVEMENT STRATEGIES

To enhance your conversion rates:

- **Personalized Approach:** Tailor your consultations and follow-ups to address each patient's specific concerns and goals related to menopause treatment.

- **Conversion Rate Optimization (CRO):** Regularly analyze your website and booking system performance to identify and address any obstacles in the conversion process. CRO (Conversion Rate Optimization) refines this using analytics.

- **Staff Incentives:** Implement a reward system for staff members who successfully convert consultations into treatments, encouraging a proactive approach to patient care.

- **Monitoring and Analytics:** Use analytics tools to track conversions from different channels and adjust your strategies accordingly.

By focusing on these strategies and consistently evaluating your performance, you can significantly improve your practice's ability to convert consultations into paying clients. This not only drives revenue growth but also ensures that you're effectively meeting the needs of women seeking menopause treatment, ultimately contributing to the success and reputation of your practice.

INCREASING SALES: MAXIMIZING VALUE THROUGH UPSELLS AND CROSS-SELLS

Increasing sales through upsells and cross-sells is a crucial strategy for growing your menopause treatment practice. This approach focuses on enhancing the value of each patient encounter by offering additional, complementary services or products that can further improve their health and well-being.

The Importance of Upsells and Cross-Sells

Maximizing the average ticket amount for each patient encounter is vital for several reasons:

- **Enhanced Patient Care:** Offering additional relevant treatments or products can provide more comprehensive care, addressing multiple aspects of a patient's health.

- **Increased Revenue:** By increasing the average transaction value, you can significantly boost your practice's revenue without necessarily increasing patient volume.

- **Improved Patient Satisfaction:** When done correctly, upsells and cross-sells can enhance the overall patient experience by providing solutions they may not have been aware of.

- **Efficient Resource Utilization:** Maximizing value from existing patients allows for better utilization of your practice's resources and staff time.

Strategies for Effective Upsells and Cross-Sells

To successfully implement upsells and cross-sells in your practice, consider the following strategies:

- **Comprehensive Treatment Plans:** Develop holistic treatment packages that address multiple aspects of menopausal health, such as hormone therapy, weight management, and aesthetics.

- **Premium Services:** Introduce high-value services like personalized genetic testing or advanced diagnostic procedures that justify higher fees.

- **Product Sales:** Offer high-quality supplements, skincare products, or other items specifically designed for menopausal women.

- **Tiered Pricing**: Implement a tiered pricing structure for different levels of care or membership, allowing patients to choose more comprehensive options.

- **Staff Training**: Equip your team with the knowledge and skills to effectively communicate the benefits of additional treatments or products.

Evaluating and Grading Your Performance

To assess the effectiveness of your upsell and cross-sell efforts, consider these key metrics:

- **Average Transaction Value**: Monitor the average amount spent by patients per visit or treatment course.

- **Upsell/Cross-sell Conversion Rate**: Track the percentage of patients who opt for additional services or products when offered.

- **Patient Satisfaction Scores**: Ensure that your upsell and cross-sell strategies are enhancing, not detracting from, patient satisfaction.

- **Revenue per Patient**: Calculate the total revenue generated per patient over a specific period.

- **Staff Performance**: Evaluate individual staff members' ability to effectively offer and explain additional services or products.

Grade your performance in this area on a scale of 1-100, with 100 being excellent. If you score below 70, it's time to refine your sales training.

CONTINUOUS IMPROVEMENT STRATEGIES

To enhance your upsell and cross-sell performance:

- **Personalized Recommendations**: Use patient data to tailor suggestions for additional treatments or products based on their specific needs and treatment history.

- **Bundled Packages:** Create attractive package deals that combine complementary services at a slight discount compared to individual pricing.

- **Staff Incentives:** Implement a reward system for staff members who successfully upsell or cross-sell, encouraging a proactive approach to patient care.

7. **Patient Education:** Provide comprehensive information about the benefits of additional treatments or products, helping patients make informed decisions.

8. **Follow-up Systems:** Implement a robust follow-up system to offer additional services or products that complement initial treatments.

By focusing on these strategies and consistently evaluating your performance, you can significantly increase the average ticket amount for each patient encounter. This not only drives revenue growth but also ensures that you're providing comprehensive care to women seeking menopause treatment, ultimately contributing to the success and reputation of your practice.

GENERATING REFERRALS AND WORD-OF-MOUTH: AMPLIFYING YOUR PRACTICE'S GROWTH

Generating referrals and fostering word-of-mouth recommendations are crucial strategies for expanding your menopause treatment practice. These methods leverage the trust and satisfaction of your existing patients and professional network to attract new clients, creating a powerful and cost-effective growth engine.

The Importance of Referrals and Word-of-Mouth

Referrals and word-of-mouth recommendations are vital for several reasons:

- **Trust and Credibility**: Patients referred by other healthcare professionals or satisfied patients come with a built-in level of trust, making them more likely to engage with your practice.

- **Cost-Effective Marketing**: Referrals are often a more cost-effective way to acquire new patients compared to traditional marketing methods.

- **Higher Quality Patients**: Referred patients tend to be more aligned with your practice's specialization and are often more committed to their treatment plans.

- **Expanded Reach**: Word-of-mouth recommendations can significantly amplify your practice's visibility, reaching potential patients who might not be exposed to your other marketing efforts.

Strategies for Generating Referrals and Word-of-Mouth

To effectively generate referrals and encourage word-of-mouth recommendations, consider implementing the following strategies:

- **Develop a Robust Referral Program**: Create a structured program that incentivizes and facilitates referrals from both patients and other healthcare providers.

- **Cultivate Professional Relationships**: Build strong connections with primary care physicians, gynecologists, and other specialists who may encounter patients needing menopause treatment.

- **Leverage Patient Satisfaction**: Encourage satisfied patients to share their experiences through testimonials, online reviews, and personal recommendations.

- **Implement a Patient Referral Incentive System**: Offer rewards or discounts to patients who refer new clients to your practice.

- **Showcase Expertise**: Host educational seminars or webinars for both patients and other healthcare providers to establish your authority in menopause treatment.

- **Optimize Online Presence**: Ensure your website and social media platforms are user-friendly and contain shareable content about menopause treatment.

EVALUATING AND GRADING YOUR PERFORMANCE

To assess the effectiveness of your referral and word-of-mouth efforts, consider these key metrics:

- **Referral Source Tracking**: Monitor which sources are providing the most referrals and focus on strengthening those relationships.

- **Referral Conversion Rate**: Track how many referred patients actually book and attend appointments.

- **Patient Acquisition Cost**: Compare the cost of acquiring patients through referrals versus other marketing methods.

- **Patient Lifetime Value**: Assess whether referred patients tend to have higher lifetime value compared to other patients.

- **Online Review Metrics**: Monitor the quantity and quality of online reviews, as these serve as a form of digital word-of-mouth.

Grade your performance in this area on a scale of 1-100, with 100 being excellent. If you score below 70, it's time to strengthen your referral networks.

CONTINUOUS IMPROVEMENT STRATEGIES

To enhance your referral and word-of-mouth performance:

- **Regular Communication**: Keep referring providers updated on patient progress and treatment outcomes.

- **Streamline Referral Process**: Continuously refine your referral process to make it as smooth as possible for both referring providers and patients.

- **Personalized Approach**: Tailor your referral requests to each provider's specific practice and patient base.

- **Reciprocate Referrals**: When appropriate, refer patients to other specialists to foster mutually beneficial relationships.

- **Measure and Analyze**: Regularly review your referral data to identify trends and opportunities for improvement.

By focusing on these strategies and consistently evaluating your performance, you can create a powerful referral and word-of-mouth engine for your menopause treatment practice. This approach not only expands your patient base but also strengthens your position within the healthcare community, ultimately leading to long-term success and improved patient care.

HOW DO YOU RANK OVERALL?

Use these guidelines to evaluate, grade, and rank your performance in each of the six steps for building a successful and profitable practice. Once each of the six steps is ranked, follow the helpful tips to focus and improve upon the areas that will have the biggest impact on your business.

Ideally, you should focus on one initiative or project at a time, two at the most. Run the program for three months then re-evaluate your grade across all six steps. When applying a focused effort on one area of improvement, you will see massive results. Then it is time to focus on the next area of weakness.

BUT ... and this is a big BUT ... don't sacrifice your strengths during the process to improve in the areas where you're weak. Don't forget to keep doing the things that you, your staff, or your market team are doing well.

What's Ahead: Next, we'll position you as the expert in women's health and menopause care.

CHAPTER 4

POSITIONING YOURSELF AS THE EXPERT IN WOMEN'S HEALTH AND MENOPAUSE TREATMENTS

THE POWER OF SPECIALIZATION IN WOMEN'S HEALTH

In the evolving landscape of healthcare, positioning yourself as an expert in a niche field is no longer an option; it's essential. For medical professionals specializing in women's health, particularly menopause and anti-aging treatments, this focus offers a unique opportunity to stand out in an underserved market. By honing in on this critical stage of life, you can establish yourself as the go-to provider for women seeking relief, guidance, and solutions. This chapter explores how emphasizing expertise in menopause treatments not only distinguishes your practice but also drives long-term success through patient loyalty, higher revenue potential, and expanded service offerings.

WHY FOCUS ON MENOPAUSE?

Menopause represents a pivotal yet often overlooked phase in women's health. Millions of women experience symptoms ranging from hormonal imbalances to emotional challenges during this transition, yet many feel underserved by traditional healthcare providers. By specializing in menopause care:

- You address an underserved market

- You attract a loyal patient base

- You differentiate from competitors

THE STRATEGY OF PREEMINENCE: BECOMING THE TRUSTED EXPERT

The Strategy of Preeminence, a marketing philosophy first introduced by marketing legend Jay Abraham, emphasizes positioning yourself as the undisputed leader in your field. When applied to menopause care, this strategy involves building trust, credibility, and authority through every aspect of your practice.

KEY STEPS TO POSITION YOURSELF AS AN EXPERT

- **Assessment (Diagnosis):** Conduct a thorough assessment of your practice as described in great detail in Chapter 2. Identify your strengths, weaknesses, opportunities, and threats. This should include a review of your current marketing strategy, sales process, operations, staffing, finances, and other key areas of your practice.

- **Create a Roadmap or Plan:** Based on the assessment, create a roadmap or plan that outlines the key steps and milestones needed to achieve the strategy of preeminence. This plan should include specific goals, objectives, timelines, and metrics for success.

- **Define Your Unique Value Proposition:** Identify your unique value proposition and how it differentiates you from competitors. This can include your specialized training, expertise, experience, unique approach, or other factors that set you apart in the marketplace. Develop one or more Signature Solutions ... specialized protocols or bundles of services designed for treating menopausal women ... to distinguish yourself from competitive offerings.

- **Develop a Content Marketing Strategy**: Create a content marketing strategy that showcases your expertise and thought leadership in the area of menopause and women's health. This can include articles, blog posts, white papers, videos, podcasts, and other forms of content that provide value to potential clients.

- **Leverage Social Proof**: Use social proof to build trust and credibility with potential clients. This can include testimonials, case studies, association memberships, board positions, awards, and other forms of social proof that demonstrate your ability to deliver results for your clients.

- **Offer Exceptional Customer Service**: Provide exceptional customer service that goes above and beyond expectations. This can include personalized attention, responsive communication, and a commitment to delivering exceptional results for every client.

- **Foster a Culture of Continuous Improvement**: Foster a culture of continuous improvement and innovation that keeps you at the forefront of the industry. This can include investing in research and development, staying up-to-date on the latest industry trends and technologies, and constantly seeking out new opportunities to add value for clients.

- **Engage in Thought Leadership**: Participate in industry events, speak at conferences, and publish articles and white papers that establish you as a thought leader in your industry.

- **Monitor and Adjust**: Continuously monitor and adjust the strategy of preeminence based on feedback, results, and changes in the industry landscape. Make adjustments as needed to ensure that you're staying ahead of competitors and delivering exceptional value to your patients.

Implementing these tactics will establish yourself as an undisputed leader and expert in the field of women's health, creating a position of preeminence that sets you apart from your local competitors.

By focusing on delivering exceptional value, providing outstanding service, and constantly innovating and improving, you can build a strong and loyal client base, achieving long-term success and growth for your practice.

THE BUSINESS BENEFITS OF SPECIALIZING IN MENOPAUSE CARE

Focusing on menopause treatments not only benefits patients but also creates significant advantages for your practice:

- **Higher Conversion Rates**: Specialized expertise attracts patients ready to commit, boosting your consultation-to-client ratio.

- **Premium Pricing**: As a recognized expert, you can command higher fees for your unique services.

- **Bundled Services**: Comprehensive packages increase average spend and encourage repeat visits.

- **Lifetime Value of Patients**: Long-term care relationships with menopausal women lead to sustained revenue over years.

EXPANDING YOUR PRACTICE THROUGH STRATEGIC ALLIANCES

Collaborating with complementary professionals can further enhance your reputation as a leader in women's health:

- Partner with other providers in your area who have the same audience but are non-competitive. We'll address the power of Strategic Alliances in a future chapter.

- Establish referral networks

- Collaborate with fitness experts or nutritionists

CONTINUOUS IMPROVEMENT: STAYING AHEAD OF THE CURVE

To maintain preeminence in menopause care:

- **Invest in Ongoing Education**: Stay current with the latest research and techniques in women's health.

- **Regularly Update Your Offerings**: Introduce new treatments or refine existing ones based on patient needs and industry trends.

- **Gather Patient Feedback**: Use insights from your clients to improve services and tailor your approach.

BUILDING A LEGACY AS A WOMEN'S HEALTH EXPERT

Specializing in menopause and women's health positions you as more than just a provider ... it establishes you as a trusted partner during one of the most transformative phases of life. By focusing on this underserved segment, you reduce competition, attract loyal patients, and create opportunities for financial growth through premium services and long-term relationships. Embrace this strategy of preeminence to elevate your practice's reputation while making a meaningful difference in the lives of women navigating menopause.

ENHANCING BRAND AWARENESS AS A LEADER IN WOMEN'S HEALTH

Here are some practical tips and guidelines for building a strong presence as the definitive "brand of choice" when women are seeking relief from their menopausal symptoms.

CONTENT: THE CORNERSTONE OF BRAND AWARENESS AND POSITIONING

Why Content Matters

Content is the foundation of your brand's online presence and a crucial tool for positioning your practice as the brand of choice in women's health and menopause treatment. High-quality, relevant content helps establish your expertise, build trust with potential patients, and improve your visibility in search engine results.

Content Marketing ... Building Authority, Credibility, and Trust

- **Identify Target Audience and Content Goals:** The first step is to design a year-long content strategy. Start by identifying your target audience and content goals. This may involve conducting market research to understand the needs and preferences of the target audience and developing a clear understanding of your content marketing goals, such as increasing website traffic, generating leads, or building brand awareness. Menopause is a broad subject with multitudes of topics. It affects tens of millions of women. There is no shortage of content to cover. Your goal is to analyze the most prevalent symptoms and conditions matched to your level of expertise, experience, and ability to treat those conditions. Then you can create content that addresses the most pressing issues and promotes your solutions.

- **Develop a Content Plan:** Once the target audience and goals have been identified, the next step is to develop a comprehensive content plan outlining the specific types of content that will be created and published over the next year. This may involve developing a content calendar, identifying key themes and topics, and creating a schedule for content creation and publication.

- **Create and Publish High-Quality Content:** The final step in implementing a year-long content strategy is to create and publish high-quality content that is designed to meet the client's goals and engage their target audience. This may involve creating a mix of different types of content, such as blog posts, social media updates, infographics, videos, and other forms of content, and using a variety of channels to distribute and promote the content, such as social media, email marketing, and other online platforms. It is important to regularly analyze and adjust the content strategy based on audience engagement, feedback, and performance metrics to ensure that the content remains relevant and effective over time.

WHAT CONTENT TO CREATE

Your content should focus on topics related to women's health, menopause, and anti-aging treatments. This includes:

- Informative articles about menopause symptoms and treatments

- Educational videos explaining hormone replacement therapy

- Blog posts addressing common concerns of menopausal women

- Infographics illustrating the stages of menopause

- Patient testimonials and success stories

WHEN TO PUBLISH CONTENT

Consistency is key in content marketing. Establish a regular publishing schedule, aiming for at least one high-quality piece of content per week. This could be a blog post, article, video, or social media update.

WHERE TO SHARE CONTENT

Distribute your content across multiple channels to maximize reach:

- Your practice's website

- Social media platforms (Facebook, Instagram, LinkedIn)

- Email newsletters

- YouTube for video content

- Professional healthcare networks and forums

- Non-profit organizations such as The Menopause Association's websites

  - MenopauseAssociation.org

  - RedefiningMenopause.com

TOPICS TO COVER

Services and Procedures:

- Hormone replacement therapy options

- Anti-aging treatments for menopausal women

- Platelet-Rich Plasma treatments such as The O-Shot Procedure

- Weight Management

- Hair Restoration

- Supplements

- Devices to treat incontinence

- Vaginal lasers

- Wellness programs for menopause management

- Aesthetic procedures to reduce fine lines and wrinkles and to replace volume loss

Conditions and Concerns:

- Common menopause symptoms and their management

- Long-term health considerations for postmenopausal women

- Mental health and menopause

- Stress Urinary Incontinence (SUI ... Stress Urinary Incontinence) and bladder leakage

- Sexual dysfunction

- Loss of Libido

- Painful sex

- Skin Laxity

- Hair loss

- Weight Gain

- Brain Fog

- Hot Flashes and Night Sweats

Education (FAQs):

- "What age does menopause typically start?"
- "How long do menopause symptoms last?"
- "Are there natural alternatives to hormone therapy?"
- Myths and misconceptions

ESTABLISHING CREDIBILITY (BRAND OF CHOICE)

To position your practice as the brand of choice:

- Join The Menopause Association and highlight your membership in your marketing material.
- Secure interviews with local media outlets to discuss menopause and women's health issues.
- Issue press releases about treatments or services your practice offers for menopausal women.

REACH (BRAND AWARENESS)

To expand your reach and increase brand awareness:

- Implement SEO (Search Engine Optimization) strategies to improve your website's visibility for menopause-related searches.
- Engage in community events focused on women's health.
- Collaborate with influencers in the health and wellness space.

TOPICS AND SCHEDULE (CALENDAR FOR RELEASE)

Create a content calendar that outlines topics and publication dates for:

- Social posts: Daily tips or facts about menopause

- Articles: Weekly blog posts on your website

- Videos: Bi-weekly educational videos on YouTube

- Email marketing: Monthly newsletters with health tips and practice updates

- Books and ebooks: Quarterly releases on specific menopause-related topics

VIDEO MARKETING: ENGAGING VISUAL CONTENT FOR BRAND BUILDING

Topics for Video Content

- "Understanding Hormone Replacement Therapy"

- "5 Exercises to Relieve Menopause Symptoms"

- "Nutrition Tips for a Smooth Menopause Transition"

- "Q&A with Dr. [Your Name]: Answering Your Menopause Questions"

Schedule and Calendar

Aim to produce one to four videos per month, maintaining a consistent release schedule.

Outline and Scripting

For each video:

- Use a One Problem, One Solution format. Don't get too complicated. Each video should address a single problem and your solution ... whether a single procedure or a bundle.

- Identify 3-5 key points to cover

- Prepare questions and answers if doing a Q&A format

- Include a clear call to action, such as "Schedule a consultation" or "Download our free menopause guide"

Optimizing Videos for YouTube and Social Media

- Use keyword-rich titles and descriptions

- Create custom thumbnails that stand out

- Include relevant tags and categorize your videos correctly

- Add closed captions for accessibility and SEO (Search Engine Optimization) benefits

RESOURCES FOR VIDEO CREATION AND OPTIMIZATION

- **Equipment**: Invest in a good quality camera, microphone, and lighting setup

- **Software**: There are many alternatives for editing including AI-based platforms that do most of the work for you.

- **Platforms**: Utilize YouTube Studio or other platforms for analytics and optimization

- **Repurposing**: Extract audio for podcasts, create blog posts from video transcripts, and share short clips on social media.

EXPANDING REACH: BRAND AWARENESS, BRAND OF CHOICE, AND TRAFFIC

- **Paid Ads**: Invest in targeted Google Ads and social media advertising to reach women searching for menopause-related information.

- **Organic SEO**: Optimize your website content for keywords related to menopause, women's health, and anti-aging treatments. SEO (Search Engine Optimization) ensures visibility.

- **Local SEO**: Ensure your Google My Business listing is complete and optimized for local searches like "menopause doctor near me".

- **Radio and TV for 90% Off**: Negotiate deals with local media outlets to trade your services for advertising spots, significantly reducing your marketing costs. The beauty of a trade is that the station will typically trade you dollar for dollar. To gain the best return, you should trade several high-ticket, high-profit treatments with low disposable costs. For example, an O-Shot procedure or a series of body contouring sessions. Add a package of gift certificates that the station can give listeners. You can trade $5000 of air time for a package of one hundred $50 gift cards. This costs you very little unless the listener redeems the gift card. If they do, you gain the chance to introduce them to your practice, profit from their treatment, and gain a long-term client ... definitely a win!

- **Email Marketing**: Build an email list and send regular newsletters with valuable content, practice updates, and special offers.

- **Social Media**: Maintain an active presence on platforms where your target audience spends time, sharing a mix of educational content and engaging posts.

- **Reviews and Reputation**: Encourage satisfied patients to leave reviews on Google, Yelp, and healthcare-specific platforms. Display these reviews prominently on your website and in marketing materials.

- **Word of Mouth and Referrals:** Implement a referral program that rewards existing patients for recommending your practice to friends and family. I'll provide more detailed information about referral programs later in the book.

- **Third-Party Sites:** List your practice on reputable healthcare directories and contribute guest articles to respected women's health websites.

- **Viral Giveaways:** Host contests or giveaways of menopause-related products or services to increase engagement and attract new potential patients.

ESTABLISHING CREDIBILITY FOR FASTER, EASIER, AND MORE PROFITABLE CONVERSIONS

- **Ebooks – Ask the Expert – 24/7 Sales Force:** Create comprehensive ebooks on topics like "The Complete Guide to Navigating Menopause" or "Anti-Aging Strategies for Menopausal Women." Offer these as free downloads in exchange for email addresses, building your list while providing value.

- **Micro Topics:** Develop a series of short, focused content pieces on specific aspects of menopause, such as "Managing Hot Flashes" or "Sleep Solutions for Menopausal Women".

- **Micro Sites:** Consider creating dedicated micro-sites for specific treatments or services, such as hormone replacement therapy, weight management, The O-Shot Procedure, or anti-aging procedures.

- **Faster, Easier Conversions:** Use clear calls-to-action throughout your content, making it easy for potential patients to schedule consultations or request more information.

- **Higher Fees:** As you establish your practice as the premier choice for menopause care, you can justify premium pricing for your specialized services and expertise.

By implementing these strategies, you'll build a strong brand presence, establish your practice as the go-to choice for menopause care, and create multiple touchpoints to attract and convert patients seeking specialized women's health services.

Understanding the Signature Solution Concept

A Signature Solution is a comprehensive, bundled protocol designed to address a specific health condition or concern. In the context of menopause care, it involves combining various treatments, services, and support mechanisms into a cohesive package that is uniquely branded and marketed by your practice. This approach offers several advantages:

- **Differentiation:** By creating a proprietary protocol, you set your practice apart from competitors who may offer standard, à la carte services.

- **Value Perception:** Bundled services are often perceived as higher value, justifying premium pricing and reducing price sensitivity among patients.

- **Expertise Showcasing:** A well-designed Signature Solution demonstrates your deep understanding of menopause and your commitment to comprehensive care.

- **Improved Patient Outcomes:** By addressing multiple aspects of menopause simultaneously, you can provide more holistic and effective treatment.

- **Streamlined Operations:** A standardized protocol can improve efficiency within your practice.

BENEFITS OF A SIGNATURE SOLUTION

- Reduce Competition and Price Shopping ...

- Convert Prospects Faster and With Less Friction ...

- Command Higher Fees and Generate Recurring Income ...

Create Your Signature Solution for Menopause Care: Elevate Your Practice and Patient Experience

Menopause care presents a unique opportunity for medical professionals to differentiate their practice and provide exceptional value to patients. By developing a Signature Solution for menopause management, healthcare providers can establish themselves as leaders in their field, attract more patients, and improve overall patient outcomes. This section will explore the concept of a Signature Solution, its benefits, and how to create and implement one effectively in your practice.

DEVELOPING YOUR MENOPAUSE SIGNATURE SOLUTION

To create an effective Signature Solution for menopause care, consider the following steps:

1. Assess Patient Needs and Market Demands:

Begin by thoroughly researching the specific needs of menopausal women in your area. Conduct surveys, analyze patient data, and stay updated on the latest menopause research. This will help you identify gaps in current care offerings and opportunities for innovation. The great aspect of targeting menopausal women is that their struggle is universal, regardless of your market area. Therefore, market research is relatively simple and straightforward.

2. Define Your Unique Approach:

Based on your expertise, experience, devices, products, and the identified needs, develop a unique approach to menopause care. This could involve:

- Combining traditional hormone therapy with cutting-edge treatments

- Integrating lifestyle interventions, such as nutrition and exercise programs

- Incorporating complementary therapies like The O-Shot Procedure for treating Stress Urinary Incontinence (SUI ... Stress Urinary Incontinence) and Sexual Dysfunction

- Offering personalized genetic testing for tailored treatment plans

3. Design the Bundle Components

Your Signature Solution should include a comprehensive set of services. Think big. If a woman with unlimited funds came to you and said ... "I don't care what it costs, I want everything you offer to make me feel better, look better, and live better" ... which services delivered over the course of a year would you recommend? Start there, then scale back services and create various packages. In your Signature Solution, consider including:

- Initial comprehensive assessment and personalized treatment plan
- Hormone therapy (if appropriate)
- Regular follow-up consultations
- Vaginal laser rejuvenation
- Nutritional counseling
- Fitness program tailored for menopausal women
- Mental health support

- Educational resources and workshops
- Access to a dedicated menopause care coordinator
- Supplements
- Aesthetic Treatments

4. Create a Compelling Brand

1. **Develop a unique name and brand identity for your Signature Solution:** This could be something like "MenoPeace Protocol" or "Vitality Transition Program." Ensure the branding resonates with your target audience and reflects the quality and comprehensiveness of your offering.

2. **Establish Pricing Strategy:** Determine a pricing structure that reflects the value of your bundled services while remaining competitive. Consider offering tiered packages or optional add-ons to cater to different patient needs and budgets.

3. **Implement Technology Solutions:** Leverage healthcare solutions and other digital tools to streamline the patient experience and improve operational efficiency. This could include:

   - Online booking systems
   - Electronic health records integration
   - Secure patient portals for communication and resource access
   - Telemedicine options for remote consultations

4. **Train Your Team:** Ensure all staff members are well-versed in your Signature Solution. This includes not only the medical aspects but also the ability to communicate the value proposition to patients effectively.

MARKETING YOUR MENOPAUSE SIGNATURE SOLUTION

To successfully promote your Signature Solution:

Develop Compelling Content: Create educational materials that highlight the unique benefits of your approach. This could include blog posts, articles, videos, and downloadable guides.

- **Leverage Social Media**: Use platforms like Facebook and Instagram to share patient testimonials, menopause tips, and information about your Signature Solution.

- **Host Educational Events**: Organize workshops or webinars to showcase your expertise and introduce potential patients to your unique protocol.

- **Partner with Local Businesses**: Collaborate with gyms, health food stores, or wellness centers to cross-promote your services.

- **Utilize Email Marketing**: Build a subscriber list and send regular newsletters with valuable content and information about your Signature Solution.

- **Optimize Your Website**: Ensure your website clearly communicates the benefits of your Signature Solution and makes it easy for patients to book consultations.

MEASURING SUCCESS AND CONTINUOUS IMPROVEMENT

To ensure the ongoing success of your Signature Solution:

- **Track Key Metrics**: Monitor patient acquisition, retention rates, and satisfaction scores.

- **Gather Patient Feedback:** Regularly solicit feedback to identify areas for improvement.

- **Stay Updated:** Continuously research the latest developments in menopause care and adjust your protocol accordingly.

- **Analyze Financial Performance:** Assess the profitability of your Signature Solution and make adjustments as needed.

Example: Dr. Sarah's MenoPeace Protocol

Dr. Sarah, a functional medicine physician specializing in menopause care, developed the "MenoPeace Protocol" as her Signature Solution. The protocol includes:

- Comprehensive initial assessment with advanced hormone testing

- Personalized treatment plan combining bioidentical hormone therapy and lifestyle interventions

- Quarterly follow-up consultations

- Personalized supplements delivered monthly or quarterly

- Access to a dedicated menopause nurse educator

- Monthly group support sessions

- Customized nutrition and exercise plans

- Mindfulness and stress reduction workshops

ADD ONS:

- Annual O-Shot Procedure for SUI (Stress Urinary Incontinence) and Sexual Dysfunction

- Emsella or similar electro-magnetic chair for strengthening the pelvic floor

- Aesthetics such as toxins and fillers

- Laser rejuvenation for the face, neck, chest, and hands

- Vein therapy

- Medical Weight Loss

- Hair Restoration

- Vaginal Laser Rejuvenation

Dr. Sarah priced her protocol at a premium compared to individual services, but patients perceived great value in the comprehensive approach.

YOUR SIGNATURE SOLUTION ...
THE KEY TO GEOMETRIC GROWTH IN YOUR PRACTICE

Creating a Signature Solution for menopause care can significantly elevate your practice, attract more patients, and improve patient outcomes. By offering a comprehensive, branded protocol, you position yourself as a leader in women's health and create a unique value proposition that sets you apart from competitors. Remember, the key to success lies in understanding your patients' needs, continuously refining your approach, and effectively communicating the benefits of your Signature Solution to your target audience.

In this chapter we covered the steps to improve your Brand Awareness and how to elevate your position as an expert in women's health, thereby placing you as the undisputed Brand of Choice in your market area.

What's Ahead: Next, we'll explore a multi-channel approach to expand your reach and drive traffic.

CHAPTER 5

EXPANDING YOUR REACH: A COMPREHENSIVE GUIDE TO TRAFFIC GENERATION AND BRAND BUILDING

In today's competitive landscape of women's health providers, generating traffic is about more than just numbers ... it's about creating meaningful connections with potential clients and establishing your practice as the go-to choice for menopause-related services. This comprehensive guide explores innovative strategies to expand your reach, build powerful brand awareness, and drive sustainable growth for your practice.

THE MULTI-CHANNEL APPROACH: YOUR PRACTICE AS A HUB

Envision your practice as a central hub with multiple spokes, each representing a different avenue for attracting clients:

1. Your Website: The Digital Welcome Mat

Your website serves as the cornerstone of your online presence. To maximize its effectiveness:

- Create an interactive, user-friendly design

- Offer valuable resources like informative articles and videos

- Implement strong calls-to-action for appointment scheduling

- Optimize for search engines to improve visibility

2. Search Engine Optimization (SEO): Dominating the Digital Landscape

SEO (Search Engine Optimization) is crucial for being discovered online. Focus on two key areas:

- **Organic SEO**: Create high-quality, relevant content that naturally ranks well in search results. This includes informative blog posts, educational videos, and compelling patient testimonials.

- **Local SEO**: Optimize your Google Business Profile and website for local searches. Aim to appear in the top 3 "mapped" results for queries like "menopause specialist near me."

    Action Tip: Prioritize your most profitable services when developing your SEO strategy.

3. Email Marketing: Nurturing Relationships and Driving Conversions

Email remains one of the most effective tools for engaging potential clients:

- Build a robust email list by offering valuable resources in exchange for sign-ups

- Segment your list for personalized communication

- Implement database reactivation campaigns with promotions and seasonal reminders

- Use email to reinforce your position as the "brand of choice"

4. Social Media: Building Community and Engagement

1. **Maximize your impact on social media with these strategies:**

   - Focus on building an organic, relevant audience rather than buying followers
   - Host viral giveaways and contests to generate excitement
   - Maintain a consistent posting schedule using a content calendar
   - Balance your content mix using the 25% Rule: Teach, Tell, Touch (emotionally connect), and Sell
   - Leverage video content on Facebook to exploit the algorithm's preferences

2. **Strategic Alliances: Leveraging Partnerships**

   Expand your reach through strategic partnerships:

   - Collaborate with complementary, non-competitive businesses
   - Offer free or discounted services to potential referral partners
   - Consider hosting "TOX parties" to generate immediate income and strengthen relationships (reference Dr. Charles Runels' course for detailed strategies)

3. **Referrals: Turning Clients into Brand Advocates**

   Harness the power of word-of-mouth marketing:

   - Implement a formal referral program with rewards
   - Consistently provide exceptional service to exceed patient expectations
   - Encourage satisfied clients to share their experiences online and with friends

4. Paid Advertising: Amplifying Your Reach

Utilize paid ads to reach a wider, targeted audience:

- Run campaigns on platforms like Google, Facebook, and Instagram
- Implement retargeting strategies to keep your practice top-of-mind
- Focus on educating your audience and addressing key buying decision factors (BITSER ... Budget, Intent, Trust, Solution, Ease, and Results)

Almost every provider in this space engages in paid advertising, so let's dig a little deeper into this process for driving more traffic to your practice.

HARNESSING THE POWER OF PAID ADVERTISING

Paid advertising is a powerful tool to generate traffic and attract potential clients. Let's explore the strategic use of paid ads to boost your business growth and maximize return on investment.

THE STRATEGIC ADVANTAGE OF PAID ADVERTISING

Paid advertising offers a unique advantage: the ability to generate traffic more rapidly than organic methods. However, it's crucial to approach this strategy with caution. Before launching any paid campaigns, ensure your business reputation is impeccable, with a minimum rating of 4 stars, preferably 4.5 or higher.

A HOLISTIC APPROACH TO BUSINESS GROWTH

Remember, there are three fundamental ways to grow your business:

- Attract more clients

- Encourage existing clients to buy more frequently

- Increase the average purchase value

While attracting new clients is important, it shouldn't be your sole focus. A balanced approach considering all three aspects will yield better results.

The Attract-Qualify-Convert Framework

Successful paid advertising follows a three-step process:

- Attract potential clients through compelling ads

- Qualify leads to ensure they're a good fit for your services

- Convert qualified leads into paying clients

Maximizing ROI with Self-Liquidating Offers

A self-liquidating offer (SLO ... Self-Liquidating Offer) is a powerful strategy to offset advertising costs. By offering a low-cost, high-value product or service, you can cover your ad spend while acquiring new leads. This approach allows you to essentially get your ads for free while building a valuable client base.

The KPI Method: Unlocking Geometric Growth

By focusing on key performance indicators (KPIs ... Key Performance Indicators) and making small, consistent improvements, you can achieve geometric growth in your business. This method demonstrates the potential for significant expansion with minimal adjustments to your current processes.

Nurturing Leads: Beyond the Initial Contact

Don't let valuable leads slip away. Implement strategies to bring potential clients into your office, such as offering vouchers, discounts, or gift cards for first and second visits. This approach helps build trust and increases the likelihood of conversion.

Advertising Your Signature Solution

Focus your paid advertising efforts on promoting your unique, high-ticket signature solution. This approach offers several benefits:

- Higher lifetime value per client

- Attracts clients seeking quality rather than bargain hunters

- Sets you apart from competitors

Five-Step Process for Advertising Success

- Create compelling ads that direct users to custom landing pages

- Implement a self-booking system for pre-appointment phone consultations

- Use effective phone scripts to qualify leads

- Direct qualified leads to an educational microsite

- Conduct in-person appointments with pre-sold, informed clients

Making Informed Decisions in Paid Advertising

When planning your paid advertising strategy, consider the following:

- Define clear goals (e.g., brand awareness, traffic generation)

- Understand the difference between intent-based and interruption marketing

- Focus on attracting long-term, high-value clients

- Recognize the distinction between relational and transactional buying modes

- Emphasize unique value propositions over discounted pricing

By positioning yourself as the expert in your market and offering unparalleled value, you can command premium prices and attract clients who prioritize quality over cost.

Additional Innovative Strategies for Maximum Impact

- **Microsites and Videos**: Develop targeted microsites and engaging video content to improve findability, credibility, and to pre-sell potential clients.

- **Storefront Optimization**: If you have a physical location, ensure clear, eye-catching signage and consider window displays to attract walk-in clients.

- **Networking Events**: Attend local events to connect with potential partners like day cares, salons, doctors, and real estate agents.

- **Omnipresence**: Add social media icons to your website and email signatures for easy access across all platforms.

By implementing these comprehensive strategies, you'll create a powerful ecosystem for engaging potential clients, nurturing relationships, and establishing your practice as the premier choice for menopause-related services in your area.

What's Ahead: Next, we'll master ethical sales to turn interest into lasting patient relationships.

CHAPTER 6

EMBRACING SALES IN WOMEN'S HEALTH: A GENTLE APPROACH

In the realm of women's health, particularly in menopause management, many medical practitioners find themselves hesitant when it comes to sales. This hesitation often arises from a desire to prioritize patient care over profit, leading to a misconception that selling is inherently unethical. However, understanding that offering beneficial treatments is an essential part of patient care can shift this perspective. This chapter provides practical strategies and ethical frameworks to help practitioners and their staff approach sales in a non-threatening, low-pressure manner.

UNDERSTANDING THE ROLE OF SALES IN HEALTHCARE

Sales in healthcare should not be viewed as a transaction but rather as an opportunity to enhance patient care. When practitioners genuinely believe in the value of their services, they have an obligation to inform patients about all available treatments that could improve their quality of life. By reframing sales as a form of patient advocacy, medical professionals can approach this aspect of their practice with confidence and integrity.

STRATEGIES FOR LOW-PRESSURE SALES

"Educate, Don't Push" and "Build Trust Through Transparency": Focus on educating patients about the various treatment options available for menopause management, delivering clear, concise information transparently to address their needs and build trust. This educational approach empowers patients to make informed decisions without feeling pressured.

- **Listen Actively:** Encourage your staff to practice active listening during consultations. Understanding patients' concerns and preferences allows for tailored recommendations that resonate with their individual circumstances. This personalized approach fosters a supportive environment where patients feel valued.

- **Create a Comfortable Environment:** Design your practice space to be welcoming and non-intimidating. A calm atmosphere can ease patient anxiety and facilitate open conversations about treatment options. Consider using soft lighting, comfortable seating, and informative brochures that patients can browse at their leisure.

- **Utilize Role-Playing Exercises:** Conduct role-playing sessions with your staff to practice various patient scenarios. This method helps build confidence in handling different objections or questions without coming off as overly aggressive or sales-driven.

- **Encourage Questions:** Foster an environment where patients feel comfortable asking questions about their health and treatment options. This dialogue not only helps clarify any misconceptions but also opens the door for discussing additional services that may benefit them.

- **Set Realistic Goals:** While it's important to have sales targets, ensure they align with ethical standards and prioritize patient satisfaction over numbers. Encourage your team to focus on the quality of interactions rather than purely on closing sales.

THE ETHICAL FRAMEWORK FOR SELLING

To navigate the delicate balance between sales and patient care, it's essential to adopt an ethical framework:

- **Patient-Centric Approach**: Always prioritize the well-being of your patients. Any recommendations made should be genuinely in their best interest.

- **Informed Consent**: Ensure that patients understand their options before making decisions. This involves providing comprehensive information about all treatments available, including potential side effects and expected outcomes.

- **Avoid High-Pressure Tactics**: Steer clear of aggressive sales tactics that may alienate patients or create discomfort. Instead, aim for a consultative approach where patients feel they are part of the decision-making process.

TRAINING STAFF FOR SUCCESS

Empowering your staff with the right tools and knowledge is crucial for effective sales practices:

- **Product Knowledge**: Equip your team with thorough knowledge about the treatments offered at your practice so they can confidently discuss benefits with patients.

- **Continuous Education**: Provide ongoing training on ethical sales practices, focusing on how to communicate effectively while maintaining integrity.

- **Feedback Mechanisms**: Implement systems for staff to share experiences and challenges related to patient interactions. This collaborative learning environment encourages growth and improvement.

BONUS: DEVELOPING A FRAMEWORK FOR "NO-STRESS" AND "NO-PRESSURE" SALES

The CLOSER Framework, as explained by Alex Hormozi, serves as a guide to selling almost any product or service, but it is particularly effective for high-ticket sales. Investing time to tailor this framework pays off for each of your high-value procedures and packages. Once developed, it is much easier to train your staff on how to convert prospects into clients.

Let's explore Alex Hormozi's CLOSER strategy with an example of how to customize the system for presenting Hormone Replacement Therapy.

CLOSER stands for:

- **Clarify**: Understand the client's motivations

- **Label**: Identify specific challenges

- **Overview**: Explore past attempts and experiences

- **Sell**: Focus on the end result, not the process

- **Explain**: Address concerns and objections

- **Reinforce**: Solidify the client's decision

EXAMPLE: Sales Framework Offering Hormone Replacement Therapy

Selling Hormone Replacement Therapy (HRT) to women navigating the turbulent waters of perimenopause and menopause demands more than a clinical pitch... it requires a deeply empathetic, strategic approach that acknowledges their struggles and offers a lifeline to reclaim their vitality.

This sales framework is crafted to guide professionals through the process of connecting with these women, addressing their unique symptoms... like hot flashes, sleepless nights, and emotional rollercoasters... and presenting HRT as a transformative solution.

Customized using Alex Hormozi's CLOSER strategy... Clarify, Label, Overview, Sell, Explain, and Reinforce... this framework adapts a proven six-step methodology to the specific needs of this demographic.

Hormozi's CLOSER approach, celebrated for its focus on understanding client motivations and framing solutions as life-enhancing, is tailored here to highlight HRT's ability to ease menopausal symptoms and restore energy, confidence, and well-being. By weaving this strategy into the sales process, the framework ensures that every conversation is compassionate, compelling, and positioned to turn prospects into empowered clients who are eager to embrace HRT as their path forward.

HRT SALES FRAMEWORK FOR PERIMENOPAUSE AND MENOPAUSE

C - Clarify Their Reason for Being Here

Start by uncovering why these women are seeking HRT... perimenopause and menopause often push them to act out of desperation or a longing to feel normal again. Open with gentle, open-ended questions:

- "What brought you here to explore Hormone Replacement Therapy today?"

- "What's been happening that made you think about this?"

- "What are you hoping to change in your daily life?"

Probe deeper:

- "Are you dealing with specific symptoms... like hot flashes, night sweats, or mood swings... that you want to address?"

- "How are your symptoms affecting your daily life? Explore their bigger picture:

- "Is this about feeling healthier, regaining your energy, or just getting through the day without feeling overwhelmed?"

- "Has this transition... perimenopause or menopause... hit you recently, maybe with symptoms creeping up or a doctor's visit that confirmed it?"

Focus on their goals:

- "What's the toughest part of this phase for you right now?"

- "If we ease that, what else would you love to feel again?"

For example, they might say, "I'm here because night sweats keep me up, and I'm too tired to enjoy time with my family."

Clarifying their "why" roots the conversation in their personal experience, setting up a sales presentation that resonates.

L - Label Their Problem

Next, name their struggle... women won't commit unless they see their symptoms as a problem HRT can solve. Reflect their concerns with understanding:

- "It sounds like you're exhausted from sleepless nights and hot flashes that won't quit."

- "It seems you're frustrated with feeling moody and foggy, like you're not yourself anymore."

Dig deeper if they're vague… if they say, "I'm just looking into options," respond, "I'm sure you wouldn't spend time on this without something bothering you… what's really been tough lately?"

If they hedge, "I'll try it and see," say, "That's a great first step, but the initial consult just maps your needs… real relief takes a tailored plan."

Recap their words: "What I'm hearing is that you're tired of night sweats and low energy stealing your days, and you want to feel steady again so you can be more productive at work and at home… right?"

Labeling validates their reality… like, "You're wrestling with a body that feels out of control, despite trying to push through"… building trust and opening the door to a solution.

O - Overview Their Past Efforts

Explore what they've tried to manage these menopausal symptoms… past struggles underscore HRT's unique power.

Ask, "This can't be the first thing you've turned to… what else have you tried?"

Use the Pain Cycle Process:

(1) "What have you done to handle these symptoms?"

(2) "How long did you try it, and how long ago?"

(3) "How did that work for you?"

(4) "What else have you attempted?"

They might mention supplements, cooling pillows, diet tweaks, yoga, over-the-counter remedies, or even antidepressants.

Dig in:

- "You've been using supplements for six months... any relief?"

- "You tried yoga last year... did it help the mood swings?" They might say, "It helped a bit, but not enough," or "The hot flashes just keep coming."

- Recap with care: "So, you've tried supplements for months, switched up your diet, even pushed through yoga, but the night sweats and fatigue won't let up."

Explain it's not their fault... hormonal shifts in perimenopause and menopause are relentless, and generic fixes can't recalibrate them. Add, "With kids, work, or just life, it's hard to keep up... and it's maddening when nothing works."

This overview positions HRT as the targeted answer they've been missing.

S - SELL THE RESULTS, NOT THE JOURNEY

Offer HRT by selling the destination... a life free of menopausal chaos... not the cost or treatment logistics.

Paint their dream:

- "Imagine sleeping through the night, waking up refreshed, and feeling calm instead of on edge," or "Picture enjoying your days again... full of energy, focus, and even intimacy... without those hot flashes holding you back."

Transition naturally:

- "Want to hear how HRT can make that real?" Highlight benefits... customized hormone therapy restores estrogen, progesterone, or testosterone balance, easing hot flashes, improving sleep, stabilizing mood, and boosting vitality within weeks.

Keep it personal:

- "This is about getting your life back, so you're not just coping but thriving."

Stress success factors:

1. A full plan... consistent therapy over months;

2. Pairing with self-care like nutrition or exercise;

3. Commitment to follow-ups for fine-tuning.

Share a story:

"Most women struggle with herbs or cooling tricks because they don't fix the hormone drop... HRT resets your balance, like turning down the heat and turning up your energy."

Sell the vision... ask, "How would it feel to be yourself again?"... keeping it emotional and question-driven.

E - EXPLAIN AWAY THEIR CONCERNS

Objections... cost, safety, spousal input, or hesitation... need compassionate handling.

For "It's too expensive and not covered by insurance," say, "It's a big step... I hear you," then reframe: "It may seem expensive since you have to pay out-of-pocket, but we may be able to customize a plan to fit your budget, and we have financing options available."

If they resist, compare: "How much have you spent on supplements or sleepless nights? This is an investment to stop the hot flashes and feel alive again... less than a daily latte. What's that worth for your next family trip or to feel energetic again at work?"

For "Is it safe?" reassure: "We utilize blood work and monitoring... it's proven safe and tailored to you."

If they say, "I need to ask my husband," reinforce: "You want relief from these symptoms for that vacation and your work... does he know how tough it's been for you?"

Ask, "What do you think he will say?

If it's cost... respond with... "doesn't he want you sleeping and smiling again?"

Offer an option... "Let's set up your next appointment... if he says no, we pause; if yes, we start."

For stalling, ask, "If cost weren't an issue, would you do it? We've got options... CareCredit, monthly payments."

Stack bonuses... add a wellness consult ($200 value), vitamin B12 shots ($300 value), or a follow-up ($500 value)... to make it irresistible.

Explain away doubts by showing that HRT's precision outperforms scattered remedies, guiding them to a confident 'yes'.

R - REINFORCE THEIR DECISION

Once they commit, lock in their trust... their confidence begins to wane within 48 hours.

Say, "Congrats... you're taking control of this transition!"

Send a personal email or video: "So glad you're with us... excited to see you thrive!"

Gift them unexpectedly... provide swag like a menopause journal or a $100 discount on skincare (even for those who don't become a new HRT client, to build loyalty).

Mail a handwritten note: "Thanks for trusting us... can't wait to help you feel amazing again!"

On their first visit, greet them warmly: "Hi [Name], this is your turning point... are you ready to feel better?"

Post-start, check in with your new client: "How's it going since we began? You're on your way!" This reinforcement... warm, thoughtful, extraordinary... ensures they feel cared for, sparking word-of-mouth and turning them into advocates who share their relief with friends.

Recap of the CLOSER Framework

This framework zeroes in on perimenopause and menopause, with expanded examples tailored to women's experiences:

- Clarify: uncovers triggers ... hot flashes, fatigue, or life demands.

- Label: names their chaos, making it real and fixable.

- Overview: contrasts past attempts with HRT's targeted relief.

- Sell: offers an emotional win ... calm, energy, normalcy.

- Explain: turns objections into reasons to act, with added value.

- Reinforce: builds loyalty with exceptional support.

This CLOSER-customized framework transforms sales into a journey of renewal, delivering relief and creating raving fans among women reclaiming their lives through menopause.

SELLING AS A SERVICE TO ENHANCE PATIENT CARE

In conclusion, embracing sales in a medical practice focused on menopause management does not mean compromising ethics or patient care. Instead, it represents an opportunity to serve patients better by ensuring they are aware of all beneficial treatments available to them.

By adopting a low-pressure, educational approach rooted in trust and transparency, practitioners can confidently guide their clients toward making informed decisions that enhance their health and well-being.

By integrating these principles into daily practice, medical professionals can transform their approach to sales from a daunting task into a natural extension of patient care ... ultimately leading to improved outcomes for both clients and practices alike.

What's Ahead: Next, we'll explore how strategic client engagement can boost sales and loyalty.

CHAPTER 7

INCREASING SALES THROUGH STRATEGIC CLIENT ENGAGEMENT

As I have reiterated throughout the book, in the pursuit of growing any business, three fundamental strategies stand out:

- Acquiring new customers

- Increasing the frequency of purchases from existing clients

- Boosting the average amount each client spends per visit

Here, we dive into the latter two ... powerful levers ... increasing purchase frequency and elevating the average transaction value ... as powerful levers to drive revenue without solely relying on expanding your client base.

By removing barriers to buying, crafting irresistible offers, and anticipating client needs, you can deepen relationships with existing customers, encouraging them to return more often and invest more each time.

These approaches not only enhance sales but also build loyalty, turning one-time buyers into lifelong advocates. Drawing from proven tactics, this chapter explores actionable methods to maximize client engagement and revenue, ensuring your business thrives by meeting customers where they are... and taking them where they want to go.

DON'T KEEP YOUR CLIENTS FROM BUYING

Removing any barriers that might prevent your clients from purchasing your services is a crucial step in increasing both the frequency of their purchases and the amount they spend. The easier and more appealing you make the process, the more likely clients are to commit ... and return.

- **Easy Booking Process:** Make it effortless for clients to book appointments. Provide a fast, intuitive online booking system, a responsive phone line staffed by friendly voices, or even a mobile app for on-the-go scheduling. For instance, a client who can secure a slot in under two minutes via their phone is far more likely to book ... and book again ... than one who struggles through a clunky process. The easier it is, the more frequently they'll engage.

- **Flexible Payment Options:** Cater to diverse preferences by offering multiple payment methods ... credit/debit cards, mobile payments like Apple Pay, or installment plans for pricier services. A woman considering a $1,000 treatment package might hesitate if limited to a lump sum but jump at the chance with a $250 monthly option. Flexibility removes friction, encouraging both initial and repeat purchases.

- **Transparent Pricing:** Be upfront about costs ... no one likes surprises at checkout. Display prices clearly on your website, in brochures, and during consultations. If a service costs $750, say so, and detail what's included. Hidden fees erode trust and deter clients from returning, while clarity builds confidence, boosting both frequency and willingness to spend more.

- **Accessible Information:** Provide comprehensive details online about your services ... treatment descriptions, expected outcomes, contraindications, and aftercare tips. A client researching a treatment who finds a thorough FAQ page is more likely to book and trust you with additional services later. Informed clients feel empowered, increasing their likelihood of frequent and higher-value purchases.

- **Customer Service**: Train your staff to answer questions with expertise and warmth. A client unsure about a new service might waver, but a knowledgeable, friendly response ... like explaining the expected results of a treatment ... can seal the deal. Stellar service builds trust, encouraging clients to return often and explore pricier options.

- **Tailored Treatments**: Offer personalized solutions based on individual needs. A client seeking hormone replacement therapy might start with supplements, but a tailored plan of HRT and a starter pack of supplements increases the value ... and the bill. Showing you care about their unique goals makes them more likely to commit regularly and invest in premium services.

- **Loyalty Programs**: Reward repeat customers with a program that offers points, discounts, or exclusive perks. A client earning a free treatment after five visits is incentivized to return sooner and spend more each time to reach that reward. Loyalty drives frequency and nudges up average spend.

- **Convenient Location and Hours**: Choose an accessible location and offer hours that fit your clients' lives ... early mornings, late evenings, or weekends. A busy mom who can pop in at 7 p.m. is more likely to book regularly and add extras, increasing her spend per visit.

- **Risk Reversal**: When feasible, price your services to offer a satisfaction guarantee or refund policy. If a client knows they'll receive a refund or a redo if a treatment doesn't deliver the expected results, they're more willing to try it and return for more. Reducing risk boosts initial purchases and encourages ongoing investment.

- **Effective Marketing**: Utilize smart marketing strategies, such as social media, email campaigns, or local ads, to highlight benefits and attract clients. A campaign showcasing smooth, glowing skin post-treatment can prompt a booking and an upsell to a package. Reaching clients effectively increases both their visit frequency and spending potential.

Most business owners unintentionally limit the amount of business their customers want to do with them. By removing these barriers ... streamlining booking, offering payment flexibility, and ensuring transparency ... you create an environment where clients feel comfortable returning often and spending more, driving sales and fostering growth.

MAKE OFFERS THEY CAN'T REFUSE

Creating irresistible propositions by guaranteeing desired results is a game-changer for increasing purchase frequency and average spend. When clients see undeniable value, they're drawn back repeatedly and willing to invest more.

- **Guaranteed Results**: Promise specific outcomes ... like a 20% reduction in fine lines after a tox series, backed by before-and-after photos or skin analysis. A client who knows her $1000 package comes with measurable and meaningful results is more likely to commit, return for maintenance, and add extras, boosting her spend.

- **Risk Reversal**: Ensure clients don't bear the loss if results fall short ... offer a refund, free follow-up treatments, or an alternative service of equal value. A $600 treatment package with a "money back" pledge reduces hesitation, encouraging frequent bookings and higher investments.

- **Future Pacing**: Help clients visualize their post-service life ... describe how a weight loss package will leave them looking better, feeling better, more energized, and healthier. Use testimonials or video demos to make it real. A client picturing the results is more likely to book regularly and upgrade to a deluxe version.

- **Value Proposition**: Highlight clear benefits ... physical (smoother skin) or emotional (boosted confidence). A $500 treatment that promises both is a no-brainer, driving repeat visits and add-ons like products, increasing the ticket size.

- **Unique Experiences**: Elevate services with luxury ... a plush robe, herbal tea, or a custom playlist. A pricey treatment in a spa-like setting feels more valuable, encouraging clients to return frequently and splurge on enhancements.

- **Personalized Packages**: Craft tailored plans, such as a $2000 to $5000 Menopause Makeover bundle that includes HRT (Hormone Replacement Therapy), The O-Shot, a Supplement package, Weight Loss, or any other combination of available treatments. Clients seeing their exact needs met are more likely to commit to multiple sessions and spend more upfront.

- **Loyalty Rewards**: Offer exclusive perks for regulars ... discounts, priority slots, or VIP events. A client earning a $50 credit after three visits returns faster and adds services to hit that reward, lifting both frequency and spend.

- **Special Promotions**: Sparingly, run value-packed deals ... a $500 treatment with a free $50 add-on. Clients bite, return for the next promo, and often tack on extras, growing their average purchase. However, I don't advocate running promotions each and every month. I have a better strategy that I'll share with if you email me at info@themenopauseframework.com. This a strategy that has produced as much as $1.6 million in sales in just 11 days.

- **Educational Content:** Share articles, videos, or workshops on treatment benefits ... like how The O-Shot combats bladder leakage while improving their sexual health. Informed clients book more often and opt for pricier options they now understand.

- **Exceptional Customer Service:** Go beyond ... offer personalized consults, follow-up calls, or a welcome gift like a scented candle. A client feeling pampered returns frequently and spends more on premium services.

You're not just selling a service but a result ... an improvement in their quality of life, a boost, a transformation. These irresistible offers pull clients back repeatedly and inspire them to spend more each time, fueling sales growth.

FUTURE PACING

Take clients forward to experience life post-service, increasing their desire to buy often and spend more. A vivid future vision locks in commitment.

- **Visualize the Outcome:** In consults, paint the picture ... "After hormone replacement therapy, you'll likely be back to your old self ... before hot flashes, brain fog, fatigue, and sleep disturbances." Use testimonials to show the results of your others. Clients envisioning their outcome tend to convert more easily, book more treatments, and add other treatments and products.

- **Storytelling:** Share stories in your marketing ... like a client who has lost 20 pounds since beginning a medical weight loss program. A client relating to that will book an appointment sooner and will increase her spend for the same results.

- **Virtual Tours:** Offer online tours of your practice ... spa-like waiting area, cozy treatment rooms, and smiling staff. A client who imagines that vibe books regularly and adds extra treatments and products, boosting their ticket size.

- **Personalized Treatment Plans**: Discuss long-term gains ... "This package will cut stress and boost energy over months." Clients commit to the journey and invest more upfront.

- **Follow-up Communications**: Post-treatment, send emails with tips and reminders ... "Expect calmer days ahead." Clients return to sustain that feeling and spend more.

- **Educational Content**: Share articles, videos or blogs on lasting benefits ... like how The O-Shot was able to eliminate bladder leakage and increase sexual pleasure. Clients understanding this will book appointments consistently and opt for higher-value plans.

You're selling a future ... a better life ... more energy, less stress, better sex, better skin, and more confidence. This vision drives frequent visits and bigger spends as clients chase that reality.

SELL THEM EVERYTHING THEY'LL EVER NEED

Position your practice as every client's one-stop shop for treating menopausal symptoms, better health, aesthetics, and wellness, encouraging regular visits and higher spends by meeting all their needs.

- **Comprehensive Service Offering**: Provide a full menu of services related to combating the effects of menopause and aging, as well as wellness consultations. A client getting everything from you returns often and spends more per visit.

- **Product Sales**: Sell skincare, supplements, or other products for home use. A $50 cream, paired with a laser treatment, increases the ticket and prompts repeat purchases.

- **Personalized Treatment Plans**: Design multi-session plans with products ... like a $1500 rejuvenation package. Clients commit long-term and spend more upfront.

- **Partnerships with Other Health Professionals**: Team up with nutritionists or fitness trainers for holistic care. A $200 consult add-on increases spend and visit frequency.

- **Continual Education and Upselling**: Train staff to explain benefits and suggest upgrades ... a $500 tox treatment becomes $1200 by adding fillers. Clients spend more and explore often.

- **Loyalty Program**: Reward trying new services ... a free $50 treatment after five visits. Clients return faster and spend more to earn it.

- **Regularly Update Your Services**: Add trending treatments like vaginal lasers, IPL (Intense Pulsed Light), hair restoration, microneedling, The O-Shot®, and PDO (Polydioxanone) threads. Clients keep coming and spend on the latest options.

You're offering results ... health, beauty, and rejuvenation. This all-in-one approach drives frequent, high-value purchases.

SELL THEM WHAT THEY WANT TO BUY

Understand their desires and deliver exactly that, boosting frequency and spend.

- **Customer Surveys and Feedback**: Ask what they love or want next ... a new treatment package emerges. Clients return for it and spend more.

- **Market Research**: Add trending services like The O-Shot®, microneedling, or IPL (Intense Pulsed Light). Clients book frequently and invest in what's popular.

- **Personalized Consultations:** Recommend tailored treatments ... a $3000 anti-aging plan. Clients commit and spend more.

- **Customized Treatment Packages:** Bundle favorites ... like a $4000 menopause revitalization package. Clients buy regularly and receive a comprehensive treatment plan.

- **Upselling and Cross-Selling:** Suggest a laser treatment with a tox or filler appointment. Clients spend more per visit.

- **Special Offers and Promotions:** Offer a $750 package with a free $100 add-on. Clients return for deals and add extras.

- **Regular Communication:** Email new offers ... a $200 treatment discount. Clients book sooner and spend more.

You're selling benefits they crave ... meeting their wants drives repeat high-value purchases.

SELL THEM WHAT THEY DON'T KNOW THEY NEED

Spot unmet needs and offer solutions, increasing visits and spend.

- **Educational Marketing:** Highlight lesser-known treatments ... like a $1200 PRP (Platelet-Rich Plasma) package to fight bladder leakage. Clients try it and return.

- **Consultations:** Ask about broader goals ... a mention of sleep issues prompts an add-on for supplements. Spend rises.

- **Staff Training:** Teach staff to identify needs ... a fatigue complaint can lead to a B-12 injection and supplement package. Clients spend more.

- **Follow-up Communications:** Suggest treatment products ... a $50 serum after a laser treatment. Clients return and buy.

- **Partnerships with Other Health Professionals**: Add a $200 nutritional consult. Spend and frequency grow.

- **Regularly Update Your Services**: Introduce new treatments and packages. Clients try it and keep coming.

You're selling hidden benefits ... uncovering needs boosts sales.

SELL THEM WHAT THEY WANT TO BUY, BUT DON'T KNOW IT YET

Anticipate desires and offer solutions first, driving frequent, big spending.

Stay Ahead of Trends: Keep up-to-date with the latest trends in the health and wellness industry, especially related to menopause, and be one of the first to offer new treatments and products. This allows you to introduce your customers to new things they didn't even know they wanted yet. Clients jump in and return often for more services.

Educational Marketing: Use your marketing materials to educate your customers about the benefits of treatments and products they may not be aware of. This can help them realize that they want something they didn't know they needed.

Personalized Consultations: During consultations, discuss your clients' overall wellness and health goals, then recommend treatments and products that can help them achieve those goals. This can help them realize that they want something they didn't know they needed. Spend spikes.

Innovative Packages: Develop innovative packages that combine various treatments and products to offer a comprehensive solution to a common problem or goal. Clients commit and spend more.

Regular Communication: Regularly communicate with your clients about your latest offerings, promotions, and events. This keeps your practice top-of-mind and encourages them to try new things. Announce a new service. Clients book fast.

Loyalty Program: Implement a loyalty program that rewards customers for trying different services and products. This encourages customers to explore your full range of offerings and discover new things they want. Frequency and spend soar.

You're selling future wants ... proactive offers fuel growth.

ACTION ITEMS TO ENSURE SUCCESS

To tie these strategies together, here are key actions to implement now.

- **Perfect and Optimize One Idea at a Time**: Focus on one good idea, perfect it, and optimize all the avenues of sustainable profit that one idea holds. Only move on to the next concept once the current one is fully developed and integrated into the business.

- **Know Your Niche**: Identify the specific segment of the market, in this case ... menopausal women, that you want to capture and then hone your unique selling proposition to a sharp edge so that you can slice off as much of that market for yourself as possible.

- **Maximize Profits From Any Asset**: This includes your sales network your client network, your employees ... everything. Strategic relationships are low cost, but they can be high impact.

- **Develop Multiple Income Sources**: Diversify your income streams to avoid relying too heavily on any one source.

- **Test Everything**: Test different aspects of your business to find what works best. This could be testing different marketing strategies, processes, or services.

- **Per Inquiry Advertising**: Use advertising mediums or marketing agencies that allow you to pay in direct proportion to the number of customer inquiries or sales generated by the ads or by the agency. This reduces your advertising risk.

- **Negotiate Better Rates for Services**: Don't be shy about trying to negotiate better lower rates for anything that you need in your practice.

This chapter's strategies ... removing barriers, crafting irresistible offers, and meeting all needs ... directly target increasing purchase frequency and average spend per visit. By making buying seamless, guaranteeing results, and anticipating desires, you create a cycle where clients return often and invest more, driving sustainable revenue.

Beyond numbers, these tactics build trust and loyalty, turning clients into advocates who amplify your reach. In a competitive market, mastering these approaches ensures your practice not only survives but also thrives, delivering value that keeps clients coming back and spending generously.

What's Ahead: Next, we'll unlock the power of referrals to spark exponential growth.

CHAPTER 8

REFERRALS

Seven Reasons Why a Systematic, Predictable, and Proactive Referral Marketing Program Can Spark Exponential Growth in Your Business

Referred clients stand out as your ideal prospects because ...

- **They make faster purchase decisions and negotiate the least ...**

  Conversion rates for word-of-mouth recommendations are 3-5X higher than those of non-referred prospects. [WOMMA ... Word of Mouth Marketing Association]

  People are 4X more likely to make a purchase when referred by a friend. [Nielsen]

- **They buy the most and buy the most often ...**

  Referred customers bring you 25% higher profit margins. [Boston Consulting Group]

  Referrals have a 16% higher average order value (AOV ...

  Average Order Value) each year. [DMA ... Direct Marketing Association and Forrester]

- **They buy the highest quality and spend the most ...**

  Customer acquisitions through referrals spend 2.5X more than the average customer. [American Marketing Association]

- **They are the most enjoyable to deal with ...**

  A referred customer is 18% more loyal than a customer acquired by other means. [Harvard Business Review]

- **They refer more people more often ...**

  Referred customers are 4X more likely to refer customers to your brand than non-referred customers. [Extole]

- **They are the least expensive to acquire ...**

  Referral leads convert 30% better than leads generated from other marketing channels [R&G Technologies]

  On average, brands generate a 6X ROI (Return on Investment) for every dollar invested in influencer marketing. [Tomoson]

- **They have a higher lifetime value ...**

  Customers referred by other customers stick around 37% longer than non-referrals. [Deloitte]

  The Lifetime Value of a referred customer is 25% higher than that of other customers. [Wharton School of Business]

GROWING YOUR PRACTICE THROUGH REFERRAL SYSTEMS

Turn Your Best Clients Into Voluntary Brand Ambassadors

Most practices claim the majority of their new clients come from referrals. While, on the surface, this is probably true, it also provides a false sense of security for several reasons.

In my experience, most businesses don't have any formal or consistent referral programs. They rely on their happy clients to tell others about their experiences. The owner is missing out on potentially doubling or tripling or quadrupling the number of people just like your clients, who also need your services.

Relying solely on referrals also limits you from acquiring more clients through paid advertising, email marketing, and other marketing efforts. Many owners forego profitable campaigns because "they don't work" or they falsely believe "all my business comes from referrals."

If your business currently enjoys a steady stream of referrals, wouldn't you like to increase that lucrative stream of business?

So, what's the easiest, most effective, least expensive way to get many more clients like the clients you value most? Get your clients to do it for you! All you have to do is systematically ask your current clients to recommend your practice to people just like themselves.

Don't Settle for Passive Referrals

Chances are, your best clients are already referring friends, family, and business associates to you from time to time. And these individuals are likely very similar to your top clients. They have similar interests, similar desires, similar purchasing habits, and similar issues, especially related to women's health and menopause. They run in the same circles ... many of their friends and co-workers are the same age and, therefore, experience the same health symptoms. Your clients refer people to you because they value the benefit you bring to their lives and they want the people they know and care about to benefit as well.

For most practices, that's the extent of their efforts. They accept the modest trickle of business these passive referrals bring in ... without ever actively soliciting referrals from their clients.

Think about the number of new clients and revenue you currently enjoy through passive referrals. Now imagine five, ten, or 20 times that amount. That's the leverage potential of a formal, "active" referral system. And the best part is a client referral program will bring you immediate results. Your clients and profits will begin to grow as soon as you implement the system.

And because they're similar to your best clients, a referral-generated client will normally spend more money and seek services more often. They're almost always the most profitable, loyal, and likable portion of your client base. Best of all, referrals are self-perpetuating ... referrals generate more referrals.

Don't Be Bashful!

Some practice owners hesitate to ask for referrals because they feel it is somehow "inappropriate." They fear clients will see it as overstepping their bounds ... getting too personal.

Don't make this mistake!

There's no reason to be embarrassed, timid, or unduly sensitive about asking your clients to direct other clients to your door. It's not only appropriate and ethical, it's your benevolent obligation. Let me explain. You've got to remember that the vast majority of your clients genuinely do have a strong, bonded relationship with you. They trust you. They trust your experience, advice, and expertise. They trust the service and treatment you deliver. They have grown dependent on achieving a high level of health, satisfaction, and well-being.

And you owe it to everybody who your clients know to at least arrange the opportunity for those people to meet you, to experience your medical philosophy, and to get your best perspective on their needs, their opportunities, and their problems, and how you can help address them.

Every satisfied client you have is in a position to know, live with, live next to, hang out with, do business with, buy from, sell to, or otherwise associate with an abundance of people who are prime target prospects for your practice. But you cannot expect your clients, on their own volition, to be responsible for or even aware of the opportunity they have to bring their friends, neighbors, coworkers, employees, employers, church members, club associates, and colleagues to your practice for you. You've got to program them and program them benevolently, not self-serving.

Respect the Benefits You Give

Remember: You cannot have an effective referral system until you first and foremost respect not only your service or practice, but also the impact, implications, improvements, results, and benefits your service has on somebody's life. You've got to be very keenly connected to what occurs in their life when they trust their health in your care.

When you adopt that operating philosophy, it's easy to make the constant generation of referrals an essential responsibility, obligation, and commitment to the families, friends, and associates of every one of your clients.

To help your clients see the connection, you need to have formalized referral systems in place. These systems must be so automatic, so continual, so authoritative, and so revered that they operate continuously and automatically for both parties.

REFERRALS IN FOUR EASY STEPS

So how do you structure a strategic referral system for your business? The options are limited only by your imagination. However, most effective referral systems have certain key elements in common. For example, the first step is to set the stage. Do a little "romancing." Here's a simple four-step process you should follow ... one you can use regardless of whether your referral request is being made in person, over the telephone, or via letter:

Step 1: Tell your best clients that you enjoy working with them more than any other client you serve and that you realize they probably associate with other people like themselves who mirror their values and qualities.

Step 2: Tell them that since they know the exact people you prefer working with, you'd like to extend to them the opportunity of referring their valued and trusted associates to you. Inform them that you would prefer their referrals over any other source of clients.

Step 3: Then help the client see a clear picture of who in their lives could benefit most effectively and naturally from your services. Tell them what kind of person they might be, where they are, what they are probably doing, and why they'd benefit by working with you. Show them what that person or entity is doing or seeking right now, so that the picture is vivid.

Step 4: Then extend a totally risk-free, totally obligation-free offer. Let them know that you are willing to confer with, review, advise, or at least talk or meet with anyone important to that client as a service to that client. In other words, offer a free (or discounted) consultation to their referral without expectation of purchase, so your client sees you as a valuable expert with whom they can put their friends or colleagues in touch.

If you follow this procedure every day to every client you talk to, serve, write to, or visit for five days straight, and you also get your key staff members to try it out, too, for five working days, you can't help but get dozens or even hundreds of new clients. It's possible to triple your business in six months or less by following a client-referral process.

OFFER A SPECIAL INCENTIVE

To make your referral program even more effective, consider tying a service or product incentive to your request for referrals. There are many creative and compelling ways to thank people for referring clients and to appreciate the business they have conducted with you in the past.

You might even consider holding a referral-generating contest, in which a substantial prize is awarded to the client who brings in the most referrals.

You should also consider offering a special bonus or reduced rate to the people your clients refer. For example, offer a $50 discount on an initial consultation for new clients referred by an existing client. Why do this? Because your clients are more likely to approach people if they can provide them with some sort of "inside deal" only available through their referral. And make it reciprocal. If you offer a $50 discount to the new prospect, reward the person who referred them with a matching $50 gift card for future services.

TRY MORE THAN ONE SYSTEM

As you're considering the many approaches you could take to generate referrals, keep this in mind: There's no rule limiting you to only one system. Why be content with just one when you know that different people are moved to action by different stimuli? Don't be afraid to try a variety of methods, as each one will appeal to people differently.

You can promote a raffle or free giveaway of one or more products or services. Participants receive additional opportunities to win by referring their contacts via email or social media. These types of viral promotions are excellent for reaching new prospects and building loyalty with your client base. There are numerous platforms available to facilitate these promotions and track the referrals. All entries are added to your database and mailing list for future promotions.

You could introduce and explain one system at or just before the point of service. You may have another instance where you call or write to clients at regular intervals each year. You might have different referral propositions or incentives depending on the season (such as Christmas) or the type of clients you are targeting.

Here's another tip: As you develop your referral system or systems, consider anyone who has ever asked you for a referral. Think about who you've responded to and how you responded. What was the incentive that drove you to action? Is there any reason you can't directly or indirectly modify that approach, that system, that process, that incentive to your practice? Absolutely no reason!

START RIGHT NOW!

Here's an easy way to start. Write down at least ten of your best clients.

Over the next two weeks, email, write, text, or call five, ten, or 20 of your best clients and tell them how much you appreciate the business they do with you. Express your gratitude for the trust they've placed in you regarding their health. Tell those highly valued people that you're trying to find more clients just like them, and you'd like their help in recruiting new clients!

Remember to treat the client with respect and appreciate the value of your service. Explain to the client why generating a continuum of referrals is integral to your ability to keep doing business the way you have. It enables you to spend less on marketing and to invest more time and money into the appropriate staffing, services, and other business aspects that ultimately benefit the client.

Give it a try. I guarantee that you'll attract more clients before the end of the month. Conceivably a lot more clients. And since it doesn't cost a thing in terms of advertising or commissions to generate substantial ongoing referral business, I hope you will jump at this chance to put one of the best, instant, no-cost, high-leverage tools to work immediately.

Don't forget: A referred client will seek a higher quality and quantity of service on average than clients acquired through general advertising or marketing. They will seek services more often. They will seek additional services to complement the initial service. They will refer more people, and they will remain clients for a longer period.

Referral-generated clients are the best category of business you can develop!

Don't delay. It's time to mobilize the latent, untapped gold mine of referrals that are just sitting idle, waiting to be unleashed upon your business. Don't let referral opportunities pass you by.

Your greatest source of new clients is your existing clients, and all you've to do is ask.

What's Ahead: Next, we'll harness strategic alliances to amplify your reach and impact.

CHAPTER 9

BUILDING STRATEGIC ALLIANCES TO GROW YOUR WOMEN'S HEALTH PRACTICE

HARNESSING PARTNERSHIPS FOR EXPONENTIAL IMPACT

As a women's health specialist ... whether you're a functional medicine physician, regenerative medicine expert, or medical spa owner ... you're uniquely positioned to transform lives, especially for women navigating menopause. Growth thrives on connection, not isolation. Strategic alliances are your gateway to amplifying your reach, enhancing your credibility, and delivering unparalleled value to your patients. This chapter explores how partnerships with like-minded businesses can fuel synergy, scalability, and sustainability in your practice, drawing on my decades of experience incorporating proven principles derived from experts like Jay Abraham to guide you. Let's explore how building a network can enhance your impact and enable you to thrive over time.

THE POWER OF STRATEGIC ALLIANCES

Synergy, Scalability, and Sustainability

Strategic alliances are more than just business deals ... they're a dynamic force for growth in your women's health practice. Here's why they matter:

- **Synergy**: When you partner with others, you create a whole greater than the sum of its parts. Imagine combining your expertise in bioidentical hormone replacement therapy (BHRT ... Bioidentical Hormone Replacement Therapy) with a nutritionist's dietary wisdom. Together, you offer menopausal women a comprehensive solution ... hormone balance plus optimized nutrition ... that neither could achieve alone. This synergy magnifies your value and attracts patients seeking holistic care.

- **Scalability**: Alliances open doors to new audiences and markets. A yoga studio partnership could introduce your menopause workshops to dozens of women who'd never heard of your clinic, scaling your reach without the heavy lift of solo marketing. Over time, these connections expand your patient base exponentially.

- **Sustainability**: Long-term success hinges on mutual benefit. By aligning with partners who share your commitment to women's wellness, you build a resilient model that endures market shifts. The greatest leverage comes from relationships where everyone wins. A sustainable alliance isn't a one-off ... it's a foundation for ongoing growth.

COLLABORATION, LEVERAGE, AND INNOVATION

Beyond these core benefits, strategic alliances thrive on three pillars that are essential to business breakthroughs:

- **Collaboration**: Teaming up isn't just smart... it's transformative. Collaborating with a dermatologist to offer anti-aging skin solutions alongside your hormone therapies creates a seamless patient experience. You tap into their strengths, they tap into yours, and together you solve more of your patients' menopause-related challenges.

- **Leverage**: Leverage is about maximizing existing assets. Your partners bring client bases, expertise, and credibility you can borrow without building from scratch. A fitness center's endorsement of your body contouring treatments leverages their trust with active women, driving referrals to your door.

- **Innovation**: Staying ahead means thinking creatively. You should seek unseen opportunities in every relationship. Partnering with a wedding planner to offer pre-event menopause-friendly beauty packages (e.g., laser treatments plus stress-relief IV drips) is an innovative twist that sets you apart from competitors stuck in traditional silos.

These principles aren't theoretical ... they're your roadmap to a thriving practice. Let's dive into how to make them work for you.

CRAFTING YOUR STRATEGIC ALLIANCE NETWORK

A Three-Step Plan for Success

Building alliances requires intention and strategy. This three-step plan will help you focus on optimizing relationships and guide you to identify, develop, and execute partnerships that grow your women's health practice.

1. Identify Potential Partners

Why It Matters: The right partners share your audience ... women seeking menopause relief, or aging women ... but offer complementary, non-competitive services.

How to Do It: Research industry groups (e.g., women's wellness associations), local businesses, and healthcare networks. Look for allies with strong reputations among your ideal patients

Example: A functional medicine physician partners with a local Pilates studio whose clients ... women 40-60 ... often complain about or ask about managing menopause symptoms.

Action: Tap the pre-existing trust others have built ... it's a goldmine. Seek partners whose patients already trust them; their endorsement carries weight.

2. Develop a Partnership Plan

Why It Matters: A clear plan aligns goals and maximizes mutual benefit.

How to Do It: Outline collaboration types ... joint workshops, co-branded content, discounts for clients, or referral swaps. Define how each partner gains (e.g., joint discounts, expanded reach).

Example: A medical spa and a nutritionist co-create a "Menopause Vitality Program," blending skin rejuvenation with dietary guidance, marketed to both client bases.

Action: Craft win-win scenarios where value multiplies. Ensure your plan offers partners something irresistible ... like access to your expertise or a discount on new patient fees.

3. Execute and Monitor Your Strategy

Why It Matters: Action and adjustment keep alliances fruitful.

How to Do It: Launch with regular partner check-ins, track metrics (e.g., referral numbers, event attendance), and tweak based on feedback.

Example: A regenerative medicine clinic and a yoga studio host monthly "Hormone Harmony" sessions. After three months, 15 new patients join the clinic, prompting a quarterly schedule increase.

Action: Test, measure, adjust ... relationships grow. Use data to spot what works (e.g., a partner's email blast doubles bookings) and scale it.

A SIX-STEP APPROACH TO NON-COMPETITIVE ALLIANCES

Tapping Into Shared Audiences

Always remember... your best prospects are already someone else's customers. This six-step approach helps you forge alliances with non-competitive partners who serve women like your target audience ... those seeking menopause solutions. It's practical, patient-focused, and primed for growth.

- **Identify Complementary Partners**: Look for businesses in health, wellness, beauty, or lifestyle sectors serving women 40+. Examples: nutritionists, fitness centers, hair salons, day spas, luxury boutiques, or holistic health clinics. **Example**: A women's health specialist partners with a massage therapist whose clients crave stress relief alongside menopause care.

- **Research Their Fit**: Dig into their business model, audience, and current partnerships. Do their clients overlap with yours? Are they open to collaboration? **Example**: A dermatologist's patients ... women seeking anti-aging ... perfectly match your BHRT (Bioidentical Hormone Replacement Therapy) offerings, and they lack hormone expertise.

- **Make the First Move Reach out with a warm introduction. Highlight mutual benefits**: "Our services complement each other ... let's help more women thrive through menopause together."

Example: A medical spa emails a yoga studio, proposing a joint wellness event to attract their shared demographic.

- **Pinpoint Collaboration Opportunities**: Suggest specific ideas: co-hosted workshops, cross-promotions, or referral programs. Focus on what benefits both. **Example**: A functional medicine physician and a nutritionist launch a "Menopause Reset" webinar gaining leads for each of you.

- **Formalize the Plan**: Agree on goals (e.g., 20 new patients each), timelines (e.g., quarterly events), and responsibilities (e.g., you provide content, they promote). **Example**: A regenerative clinic and a fitness center set a 6-month referral goal, tracking progress monthly.

- **Evaluate and Evolve**: Monitor results (e.g., referral conversions), gather patient feedback, and adjust. If a partnership lags, pivot ... maybe swap a flyer campaign for a live demo. **Example**: After a Pilates studio's referrals dip, the partners add a free trial class with a menopause consult, doubling interest.

- **Bonus Action**: Don't just connect ... expand. Once one alliance succeeds, connect your partner to another ally (e.g., a nutritionist to a spa), creating a web of growth.

POTENTIAL STRATEGIC ALLIANCE PARTNERS

Here is a curated list of 20 non-competitive potential partners that serve women interested in menopause care, anti-aging, beauty, and wellness. Each offers unique collaboration potential, with examples to spark ideas. Look for ways to leverage every relationship's hidden value.

- **Hair Salons**: Clients seeking beauty enhancements could benefit from your anti-aging treatments. Example: Co-offer a "Glow Inside and Out" package with styling and BHRT consults.

Stylists are often the first to notice when menopausal women experience hair loss and are open to hair restoration procedures.

- **Dermatologists**: Referrals for skin-focused menopause solutions like PRP (Platelet-Rich Plasma) therapy. Example: Jointly host a "Skin & Hormones" seminar.

- **Plastic Surgeons**: Patients wanting non-surgical options post-procedure could try your services. Example: Cross-refer for laser skin tightening.

- **Fitness Centers**: Active women might seek body contouring or energy boosts. Example: Promote a "Fit at 50" challenge with your IV drips.

- **Nutritionists/Dietitians**: Pair dietary plans with your hormone therapies. Example: Co-create a menopause nutrition guide.

- **Chiropractors**: Clients with tension could benefit from your stress-relief treatments. Example: Offer a combo massage and hormone check.

- **Yoga/Pilates Studios**: Holistic-minded women align with your wellness focus. Example: Host a "Menopause Yoga" series with consults.

- **Massage Therapists**: Relaxation seekers could explore your spa services. Example: Bundle massages with facials for menopause relief.

- **Estheticians**: Facial treatment clients might need your deeper anti-aging expertise. Example: Refer for microneedling after peels.

- **Holistic Health Centers**: Alternative therapy fans could try your regenerative options. Example: Partner on an "Energy Reset" day with acupuncture and peptides.

- **Ophthalmologists/Optometrists:** Eye-area enhancements (e.g., Botox) complement their work. Example: Co-promote an "Eyes & Face" beauty event.

- **Photographers:** Clients booking portrait sessions could enhance their look with your treatments. Example: Create a 'Photo-Ready Skin' package with a pre-shoot facial, laser treatments, or Botox.

- **Wedding Planners:** Brides or mothers could prep with menopause-friendly beauty. Example: Create a "Wedding Wellness" package.

- **Personal Stylists:** Makeover clients might seek skin and hormone upgrades. xample: Co-host a "Total Transformation" workshop.

- **Event Planners:** Corporate wellness events could feature your services. Example: Provide mini-consults at a women's conference.

- **Resorts:** Guests seeking relaxation could enjoy your spa or wellness offerings. Example: Partner on a "Menopause Escape" package with hormone consults and spa days.

- **Orthopedic Surgeons:** Post-op patients might need recovery boosts. Example: Refer for IV therapy to aid healing.

- **Dental Offices:** Cosmetic dentistry clients could explore facial aesthetics. Example: Co-market a "Smile & Skin" package.

- **Boutique Hotels:** Vacationers might indulge in your spa offerings. Example: Partner on a "Menopause Retreat" weekend.

- **Day Spas:** Clients enjoying pampering could upgrade with your medical-grade treatments. Example: Combine their massages with your anti-aging IV drips for a "Total Rejuvenation" day.

BUILDING THE BRIDGE

When approaching these partners, lead with value. Offer them an irresistible yes. Provide incentives (e.g., free treatments, discounts, co-branded perks) and emphasize mutual growth: "Our patients overlap … let's double our impact." Strong relationships, rooted in trust and reciprocity, transform these alliances into gold mines.

PUTTING IT INTO PRACTICE – YOUR STRATEGIC ALLIANCE BLUEPRINT

Ready to act? Here's how to start:

- **Pick Three Partners**: From the list above, choose three that align with your menopause focus. Why them? What can you offer?

- **Craft Your Pitch**: Write a 2-3 sentence intro highlighting mutual benefits. Example: "Our BHRT expertise complements your yoga classes … let's co-host a wellness event for menopausal women."

- **Set One Goal**: Aim for a specific outcome in 90 days (e.g., 10 referrals, a sold-out workshop).

- **Track and Tweak**: After one month, check progress. If it's slow, add a perk (e.g., free trial) or shift focus.

- **Final Insight**: Your success lies in the follow-through. Don't just start alliances … nurture them. A thriving network of partners can multiply your practice's reach, revenue, and reputation for years to come.

What's Ahead: Next, we'll tie it all together with a roadmap to launch your thriving practice.

CHAPTER 10

BRINGING IT ALL TOGETHER – YOUR ROADMAP TO A THRIVING MENOPAUSE PRACTICE

Congratulations! You've journeyed through the pages of this book, uncovering the untapped potential of menopause care and the proven strategies to build a thriving, cash-based practice that transforms women's lives. As a medical professional specializing in women's health ... whether you're a functional medicine physician, regenerative medicine expert, or medical spa owner ... you're now equipped with a comprehensive toolkit to serve the millions of women navigating menopause while growing a sustainable, profitable business. This final chapter ties together the key lessons from our exploration, offering a clear roadmap to put these ideas into action and cement your legacy in this underserved field.

THE VISION: A GOLDEN OPPORTUNITY REALIZED

In Chapter 1, we set the stage with a powerful truth: menopause care is a vast, growing market crying out for specialized attention. With over 1 billion postmenopausal women worldwide by 2025 and 6,000 U.S. women entering menopause daily, the demand is undeniable ... yet only 1 in 5 receive a referral to a specialist, and 75% of those seeking help go untreated. This gap isn't just a healthcare failing; it's your golden opportunity. Menopause isn't a footnote ... it's a pivotal life stage affecting women's quality of life, careers, and relationships, costing $1.8 billion annually in lost productivity. By stepping into this space, you tap into a $24.4 billion market by 2030, offering cash-based services like hormone therapy, vaginal rejuvenation, and aesthetic treatments that meet women where they are and deliver life-changing results.

But it's more than numbers. Women, who drive 80% of U.S. healthcare decisions, aren't just patients ... they're gateways to families and communities. Build trust with them, and your practice becomes a hub of influence, expanding beyond menopause to serve broader needs. This isn't just a vision ... it's your call to lead to action you've answered by reading this book.

THE FUNDAMENTALS: THREE PILLARS OF GROWTH

Chapter 2 introduced the bedrock of your success: Jay Abraham's three ways to grow any business ... acquiring more clients, increasing average purchase value, and boosting purchase frequency. These aren't abstract theories; they're your levers for geometric growth. A 10% improvement in each ... say, from 1,200 clients at $500 per visit twice a year to 1,320 clients at $550 per visit 2.2 times a year ... jumps revenue from $1.2 million to nearly $1.6 million, a 33% leap. For your menopause practice, this means blending targeted marketing (Chapter 1's online presence), comprehensive treatment plans (Chapter 7's packages), and ongoing care programs (Chapter 6's follow-ups) to maximize every patient relationship. Exceptional value at every step ensures these pillars don't just grow revenue ... they deepen impact.

THE STRATEGY: SIX STEPS TO PREDICTABLE SUCCESS

Chapter 2 also laid out the six-step patient journey ... building brand awareness, becoming the brand of choice, creating traffic, converting consultations, increasing sales, and generating referrals. These steps, detailed further in Chapters 6-8, form your strategic backbone. Start with awareness (Chapter 3's SEO ... Search Engine Optimization ... and content marketing) to make your menopause expertise known. Position yourself as the go-to provider (Chapter 6's trust-building) to stand out in a sea of generalists. Drive traffic (Chapter 4's paid ads) and convert it (Chapter 6's low-pressure sales) to turn interest into bookings. Then, boost sales (Chapter 7's upselling) and harness referrals (Chapter 8's systems) to fuel exponential growth. Each step flows into the next, creating a cycle where satisfied patients become your loudest advocates.

THE EVALUATION: NEVER WASTE A DOLLAR AGAIN

Chapter 3 taught you to treat your practice like a patient ... examine, diagnose, and treat inefficiencies. Scoring yourself on client acquisition, average spend, and visit frequency (1-100, with 70+ as the goal) reveals strengths and weaknesses. Ranking the six steps (Chapter 2) from 1-6 and multiplying by 5% prioritizes your focus ... say, 30% on increasing sales if upselling lags. This lens ensures every marketing dollar targets your weakest links, like boosting traffic (Chapter 4) before refining conversions (Chapter 6). Continuous grading keeps your practice lean and effective, maximizing return on investment.

THE MINDSET: SALES AS SERVICE

Chapter 6 reframed sales from a pushy chore to a gentle act of care. In menopause management, offering treatments like HRT (Hormone Replacement Therapy) or laser therapies isn't about profit ... it's about advocacy. Educate without pressure, listen actively, and build trust (the CLOSER framework's Clarify and Label steps) to uncover needs. Sell the vision (Sell step) of restored energy and confidence, not just the process, and reinforce decisions (Reinforce step) with warmth. This ethical approach turns consultations into partnerships, increasing purchase frequency and value as patients embrace comprehensive care they trust.

THE ENGAGEMENT: DEEPENING CLIENT RELATIONSHIPS

Chapter 7 showed how removing barriers ... easy booking, flexible payments, transparent pricing ... drives frequent visits. Irresistible offers (guaranteed results, risk reversal) and future pacing (vivid outcomes) boost average spend. Meeting all needs ... comprehensive services, personalized plans ... and anticipating desires (trending treatments like The O-Shot®) ensure clients see you as their one-stop solution. A client booking a $2,000 menopause package returns quarterly and adds $500 in products because you've made it seamless, valuable, and tailored. Loyalty programs and exceptional service seal the deal, turning clients into regulars.

THE AMPLIFIERS: REFERRALS AND ALLIANCES

Chapters 8 and 9 unleashed your growth accelerators. Referral systems (Chapter 8) turn happy clients into ambassadors ... referred patients convert 3-5X faster, spend 2.5X more, and stay 37% longer. The four-step process ... praise, invite, describe, offer ... plus incentives like $50 discounts doubles your reach overnight. Strategic alliances (Chapter 9) multiply this impact. Partner with yoga studios, nutritionists, or day spas to tap shared audiences, leveraging their trust (synergy) to scale your reach and sustain growth. A "Menopause Vitality Program" with a dermatologist blends expertise, drawing dozens of new patients without solo effort.

YOUR ROADMAP: ACTION STEPS TO THRIVE

Here's your step-by-step plan to launch today. You've got the vision, tools, and strategies ... now it's time to act. Here's your roadmap to integrate these lessons and build a menopause practice that thrives:

1. **Define Your Niche (Chapter 1)**

    Brand yourself as *the* menopause expert. Update your website and social media with "Menopause Care Specialist" messaging. Join The Menopause Association to boost credibility and network with allies.

2. **Assess Your Baseline (Chapter 3)**

    Score your practice on the three growth pillars and six steps today. Identify your top three focus areas (e.g., traffic at 25%, sales at 20%). Allocate time and budget here first ... say, 30% on upselling training.

3. **Launch Core Systems (Chapters 6-7)**

    Implement an online booking system and a $50 referral incentive program (Chapter 8's four steps). Craft a $2,000 menopause package (Chapter 7) with HRT (Hormone Replacement Therapy), nutrition counseling, and a free consult to boost spend and frequency.

4. **Forge Three Alliances (Chapter 9)**

    Pick three partners from the 20 listed ... say, a yoga studio, nutritionist, and day spa. Pitch a co-hosted "Hormone Harmony" event within 90 days, aiming for 15 new patients each. Track referrals monthly.

5. **Amplify with Marketing (Chapter 4)**

   Start a blog on menopause myths and run a $500/month Google Ads campaign targeting "menopause relief [your city]." Use Chapter 6's CLOSER framework in consults to convert 20% more leads.

6. **Monitor and Refine (Chapter 3)**

   Review KPIs (Key Performance Indicators ... e.g., leads, conversions, ROAS ... Return on Ad Spend) every 30 days. If traffic lags, tweak ads; if referrals dip, add a contest. Aim to move each weak step up one rank by your next self-assessment.

THE PAYOFF: IMPACT AND LEGACY

Envision this: In six months, your practice hums with 50 new referral patients monthly, each spending $1,000+ on tailored plans. Your alliances fill workshops, and your online presence draws women nationwide. Revenue climbs past $2 million annually, but the real win is deeper ... women reclaim vitality, confidence, and joy because of you. You've not only built a business; you've reshaped menopause care, proving it's not just aging ... it's a vibrant new chapter.

This isn't the end ... it's your beginning. The menopause market awaits, vast and underserved. With every strategy you've learned, from ethical sales to strategic partnerships, you're ready to lead. Step forward, act boldly, and watch your practice ... and your patients ... thrive. Share your success with me at info@themenopauseframework.com. I can't wait to hear how you're transforming lives, one woman at a time.

RESOURCES

THE MENOPAUSE FRAMEWORK:

TheMenopauseFramework.com

Training and consulting for you and your staff.

3-Day in-person and 8-week virtual training events.

On-going support.

THE MENOPAUSE ASSOCIATION:

MenopauseAssociation.org

RedefiningMenopause.com

The Menopause Association, a 501(c)(3) nonprofit, connects women with expert medical providers specializing in menopause care, offering a functional and integrative approach to treatment. Our mission is to educate, empower, and provide resources for women so they may make informed health decisions during menopause while offering compassionate support throughout the aging process.

APPLY TO SERVE ON THE MENOPAUSE ASSOCIATION ADVISORY BOARD:

- Do you have a passion for women's health and a commitment to improving the menopausal journey?

- Are you a medical professional eager to share your expertise on menopause-related issues?

- Do you want to be a nationally recognized authority in menopausal care and lead innovations in women's health?

- Are you dedicated to elevating your career as a menopause specialist and enhancing the reputation of yourself and your practice?

- Can you see yourself shaping the future of menopause care and influencing positive change?

- We invite you to join a community of dedicated healthcare professionals who share a common goal: to empower women and redefine the menopause experience.

Scan or go to https://fstlnk.com/Nwts9K

THE CELLULAR MEDICINE ASSOCIATION:

CellularMedicineAssociation.org

The Cellular Medicine Association (CMA) is a beacon of innovation in healthcare led by the esteemed Dr. Charles Runels. The CMA is dedicated to advancing the practice of cellular medicine through rigorous research, education, and a commitment to excellence in patient care. The CMA is a collaborative network where pioneering physicians come together to explore the frontiers of medical science and translate groundbreaking discoveries into life-changing treatments.

TRAINING FOR PRP INJECTIONS:

TrainingForPRP.com

Online and in-person training and certification by Dr. Charles Runels, inventor of The O-Shot® Procedure, The P-Shot Procedure®, The Vampire Facelift®, The Vampire Facial®, The Vampire Breast Lift®, Vampire Hair Restoration®.

Receive a Free Preview Package with physical samples of products, printed books, and a binder of materials so you can best evaluate the latest scientific research related to the procedures presented through The Cellular Medicine Association.

BHRT TRAINING ACADEMY:

BHRTTrainingAcademy.com

The BHRT Training Academy was established to equip healthcare providers with essential training in bioidentical hormone replacement therapy. Enhance Patient Care and Grow Your Practice in the Flourishing $9 billion Bioidentical Hormone Replacement Therapy Market.

PLATINUM MEDIA SOLUTIONS:

PlatinumMediaSolutions.com

Platinum Media Solutions specializes in crafting bespoke strategies to help businesses excel in the competitive market, offering a suite of services from strategic planning to digital marketing, all rooted in deep industry knowledge. Their commitment to excellence and collaborative approach ensures personalized solutions that align with each client's unique goals for sustainable growth and success.

NUTRAFI:

NUTRAFi.com

NUTRAFi is your trusted wholesaler of oral vitamin sprays. Their revolutionary nutritional supplement sprays are up to 90% effective. More than traditional pill, powder, and gummy supplements. Increase your revenue with these high-demand products.

DR. CHARLES RUNELS – TOX SECRETS AND PROFITABLE TOX PARTIES

BotoxClass.com

Learn how to create beautiful results with botulinum neurotoxin (bont), how to use bont to treat difficult problems (like bruxism, depression, ed, and migraines), and how to fill their office with people who want those treatments.

Scan to Order or go to https://fstlnk.com/8twwbh

FREE REPORT: SYSTEMATICALLY ATTRACT MORE CLIENTS WITH THE O-SHOT® PROCEDURE

An easy framework to consistently and predictably secure more high-value clients with the O-Shot® Procedure... Even on a limited budget... Without spending on ads!

Scan or go to https://fstlnk.com/5sr1bw

HEALTHSPAN ACTION COALITION:

HealthspanAction.org

Founded by Bernard Siegel, Melissa King, and Sabrina Cohen, with the goal of leading a new public policy coalition concerned about Healthspan issues that affect all human beings, both young and old. Through this movement, the coalition aims to help address the need for accelerating, broadening, and expanding access to new government-approved medical advancements that could positively impact the lives of all people, ultimately achieving a higher quality of life and improved health for all humanity.

www.ingramcontent.com/pod-product-compliance
Lightning Source LLC
Chambersburg PA
CBHW072255270326
41930CB00010B/2387